INNER SPACE
AWAKENING
THROUGH ART AND POETRY

By:

Mother licensed psychotherapist and her artist daughter.

(With NSA Signature Status, from the National Society of Artists, in U.S.A.)

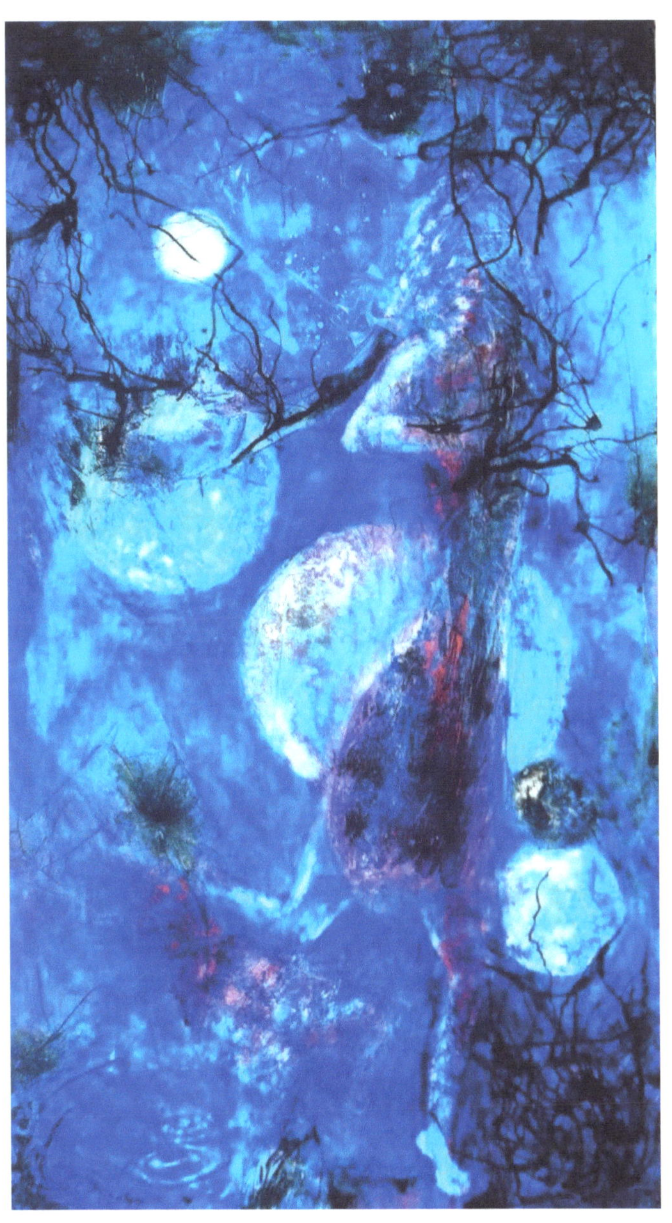

Teresa Piqué Algaze Espinoza
M.S.W. L.C.S.W.

Eugenia Algaze Garcia
B.B.A. M.B.A. N.S.A.

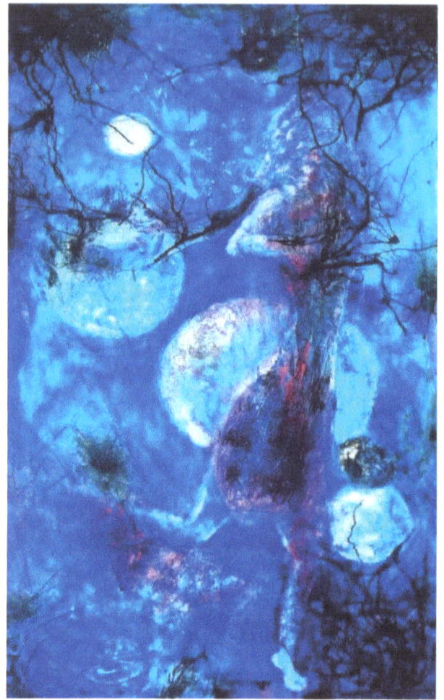

Running Between Worlds
12x24 India Ink on claybord, © 2013

This artwork, was selected to represents the inner state of all who are living in this period in history where the degree of conflicts at different levels: (individual, financial social, racial, religious, political, or a mix of them, has reached a point of extreme preoccupation. Changes are needed at the individual, national, and international levels to improve the quality of life of each human being, and the environment that sustains each one of them. This artwork is also a self -portrait of the artist that reflects how it felt to be running between many different "worlds" with the responsibilities of being a wife, a mom, a daughter, chauffer, a cook, a volunteer, an artist, a business owner, a friend, and more, finding a balance, while preserving quality of everything done, with a sharp focus in time management and purpose.

<u>**A PREAMBLE**</u>

This book is structured as a concrete poem: <u>"The In-Between"</u> reflecting a theme in free verse with a third person omniscient point of view. It shows some of the concepts that lay hidden in-between our thoughts. These small but loaded extracts, show our present way of thinking and highlight consequences, while at the same time, stimulating and inspiring the mind. Nestled in a framework of alternating, colorful and thought-provoking paintings the reader will enjoy, a unique, absorbing, stimulating experience. The writer, is a licensed multicultural and multilingual psychotherapist, who has heightened her discernment through many years of personal and professional exposures to the human condition. Her daughter Eugenia's art presents the wisdom of another highly educated, professional, creative woman who through more than 4 decades of inspiration, effort and tenacity, has practiced to reflect her creative perspectives through her Mindful-Art paintings.

<u>**A DEDICATION**</u>

To the space between our thoughts, that fruitful silence which is
the birthplace of infinite ideas
and hurricanes of understanding;
To the essence of humanity in its constant striving for
justice and survival,
if rooted and established in love.

<u>**BOOK TITLE**</u>

INNER SPACE
AWAKENING
THROUGH ART AND POETRY
A collaboration between: A licensed Psychotherapist
&
her daughter,
an artist with Signature Award, from
The National Society of Artists
© 2024.

<u>**CONTENT:**</u>

THOUGHT EXPRESSIONS
TO STIMULATE
THE CONCEPTION OF CREATIVE SOLUTIONS
THROUGH
ART AND FREE VERSE POETRY

BY:

TERESA PIQUÉ ALGAZE – ESPINOZA   M.S.W. L.C.S.W.
EUGENIA ALGAZE GARCIA   B.B.A. M.B.A. N.S.A.

AUTHOR'S NOTE

♈♈

The reason for this art and thoughts collage is to stimulate that state of awareness that can propel the enlightened reader to act in good will for the benefit of the common good. It awakens when we explore, in depth, what we think and do. It is a moment in time loaded with potential benefits with the power of influencing our perceptions, our established habits, and automatic actions. It is from that internal state of being that we can see new perspectives about ourselves and our present human condition; study the possibilities; and do what we can do, today, to start, bring, or be, an individual or collective solution. The goals of this book, while exploring the depth of inner space are to:

- AWAKEN THE NEED FOR INQUIRY ABOUT YOUR PRESENT ROLE IN THE WORLD.

- SPARK A NEED TO FOCUS ON THE DISPARITIES THAT CAUSE PAIN AND SUFFEREING AND RECOGNIZE THE POWER AVAILABLE FOR YOU TO BE A SPECIAL MICRO OR MACRO INFLUENCE FOR RELIEF.

- ASSIST IN HELPING YOU CONNECT CONCIENCE, KNOWLEDGE AND HUMAN NEEDS TO BECOME A TOOL FOR CHANGE WHILE EXPERIENCING A SPIRITUAL AND MENTAL ENLIGHTENMENT THROUGH ART AND FREE VERSE POETRY.

- RECOGNIZE OUR HUMAN ABILITY TO LOVE, SHARE, COOPERATE AND LIVE IN HARMONY.

- DIRECT YOUR THOUGHTS TOWARD THE POSSIBILITY OF A JUST HUMANITY.

<u>TABLE OF CONTENTS</u>

🏆🏆

English in Black　　🏆🏆　　Español en color azul

BIBLIOGRAPHY

☙❧

<u>Holy Bible</u>, King James Version ©1960 Holman Bible Publishers. Used with permission: Isa. 60:1; I Ths. 3:12; Ps. 3:5; Col. 1:21; Job 37:16; Isa. 44:3; Prv. 3:6; Ps. 67:4; 2 Cor. 4:18; Job 31:6; Ps. 119:159; Ps. 18:28; Mt. 25:45, 46; Ezq.17:10.

Al-Nawawi, El Iman. <u>The Way Toward Paradise. Sayings by Muhammad God's Messenger.</u> Second Edition 1995. Amana Publications 1994. Quote from The Sacred Koran (11:6) Chapter 53, Pg. 83.

Gibran, Kahlil, <u>The Prophet.</u> First Edition: 1926. 31st Printing 1991 Published by Alfred A Knopf, Inc. Pg. 38.

Heine, Vivian L. LMSW- ACP LSOTP & Lewis, Diana G. LPC, LSOTP <u>Ventura Manual</u> Pgs.30-38. Used with permission.

Shakespeare, William. <u>Hamlet.</u> Act iii Es.1.

Wikipedia. Text under CC- BY- SA license. "Ubuntu" definition.

MINDFUL ART

❦❦

Art that recognizes reality in different forms.
Art that explores and expands the imagination through awareness.
"The Longer You Look..., The More You See."

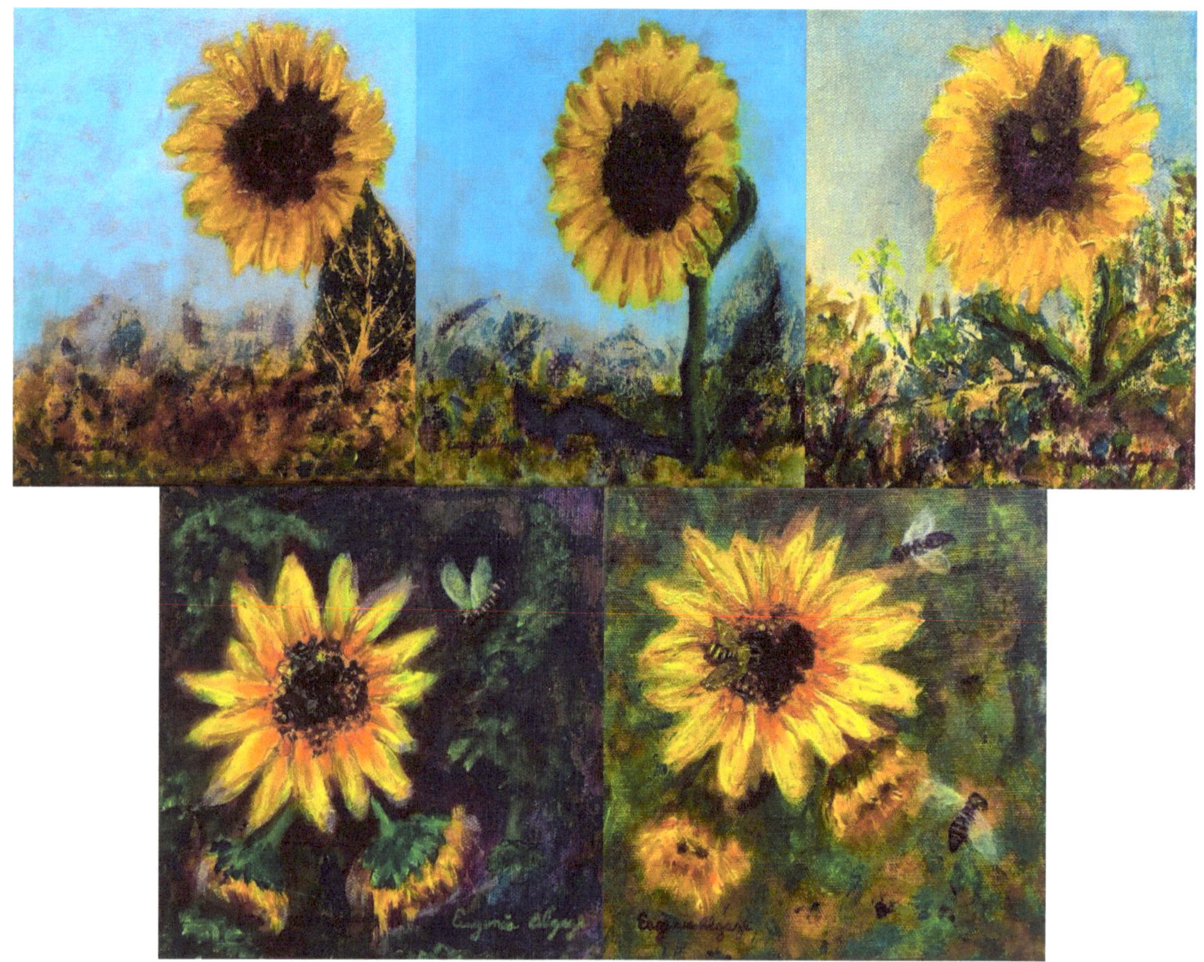

THE SUNFLOWER SERIES   © 2023
www.mindful-art.com
www.facebook.com/Mindful.Art.Eugenia.Algaze.Garcia

"LETTING LOVE SHINE"

❦❦

Isa. 60:1

"ARISE, SHINE FOR THY LIGHT IS COME AND THE GLORY OF THE LORD IS
RISEN UPON THEE."

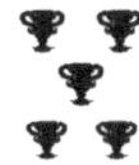

<u>THE IN-BETWEEN</u>

(A FREE VERSE POEM)

By:

Teresa Pique Algaze Espinoza LMSW LCSW

© 2024

<u>ON OUR SPIRITUAL ESSENCE</u>

****

BETWEEN POETRY AND PROSE
THE PRISON OF RHYME.

BETWEEN INSPIRATION AND A POEM
CONTACT WITH THE WATER THAT FLOWS IN THE RIVER OF SILENCE,
A TOAST AND A SONG.

BETWEEN SUNRISE AND SUNSET
THE START OF A DAY, THE END OF A NIGHT,
THE PASSING OF TIME IN ITS DAILY PARADE
WITH HUMANITY:
SOME SUFFERING OTHERS REJOYCING, AND ALREADY MANY
LOOKING FOR HOW TO IMPROVE.

BETWEEN BEING AND LIVING
THE GIFT OF A BREATH OF LIFE.
LIKE LIGHT AND WATER OPEN UP A SEED,
LIFE AND LOVE, CREATE AN IDENTITY.
ALL GIFTS FROM OUR CREATOR.

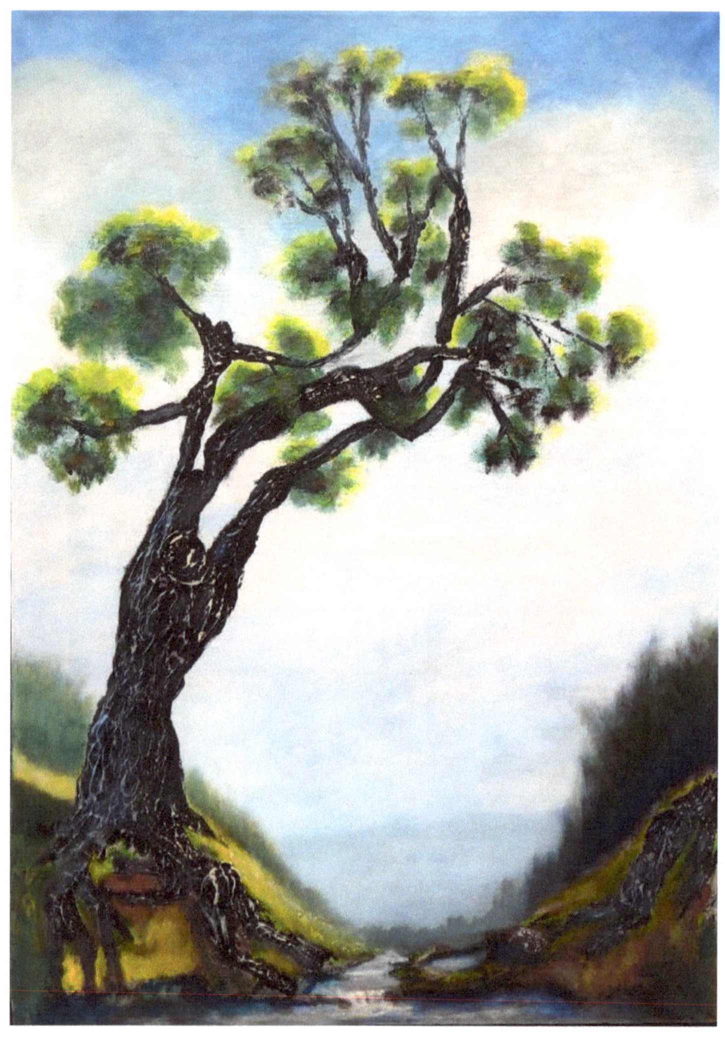

UBUNTU

Ubuntu: "I am, because we are".

"Ubuntu is a word from a Southern African language that means humanity or humanness. It is a social philosophy, an ethic and a world view. It promotes the obligation and responsibility of humans towards the welfare of one another and to the environment. It is based on the belief that a person is a person through others and that humanity is a product of socialization and good social values. It implies equality and dignity. These values and practices make people authentic human beings where their sense of self is shaped by their relationship to others"

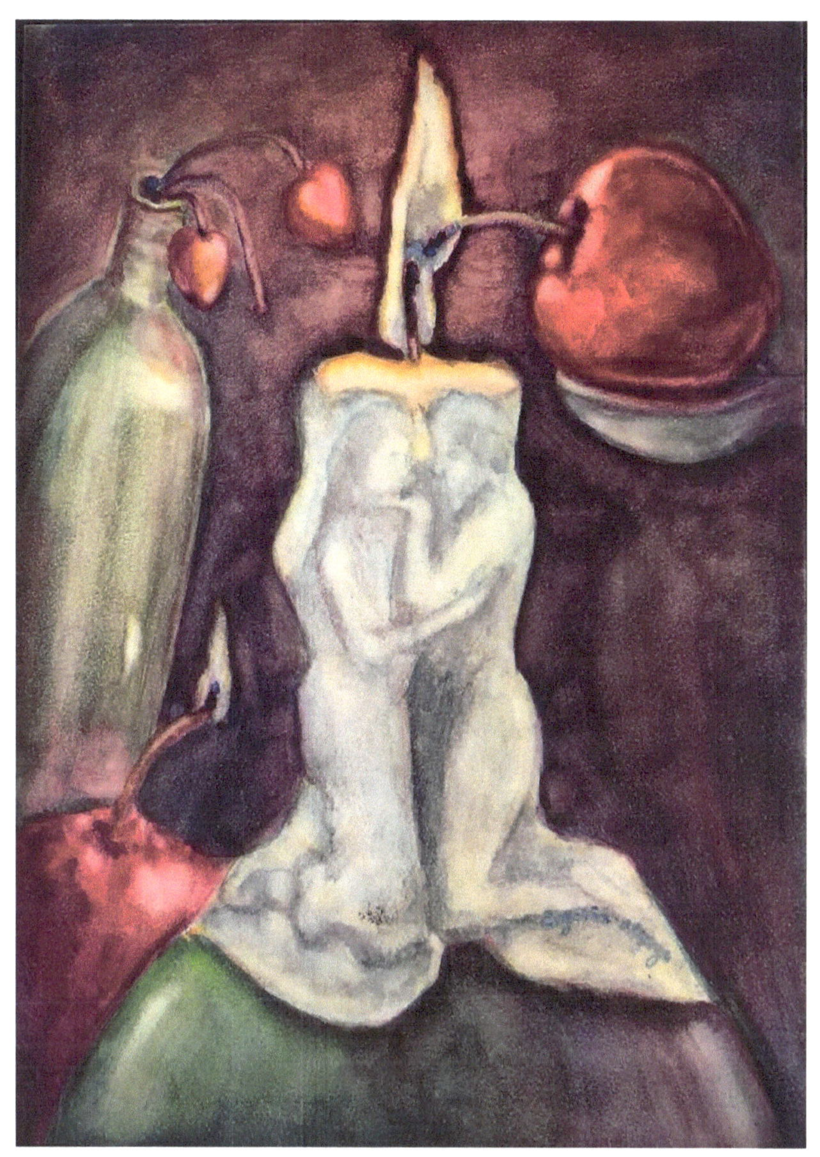

RE-KINDLED SPIRITS

♈ ♈

I Ths. 3:12

"AND THE LORD MAKE YOU TO INCREASE AND ABOUND IN LOVE ONE TOWARD
ANOTHER, AND TOWARD ALL MEN, EVEN AS WE DO TOWARD YOU".

****

BETWEEN REASON AND PASSION
THE BATTLEFIELD OF THE SOUL.
(HORMONES & ADRENALINE VS. LOGIC AND MORALS).

BETWEEN TWO HEARTS
THERE ARE MILLIONS OF ILLUSIONS, DREAMS, AND HOPES.
REALITY SYNCHRONIZES OR DESYNCHRONIZES THEIR HEARTBEAT.

BETWEEN TWO HARMONIC SOULS
A COSMOS OF JOY.

BETWEEN TWO DESYNCRONIZED BEINGS
A MOUNTAIN OF CONFLICTS
WITH
MANY POSSIBILITIES FOR SOLUTIONS.

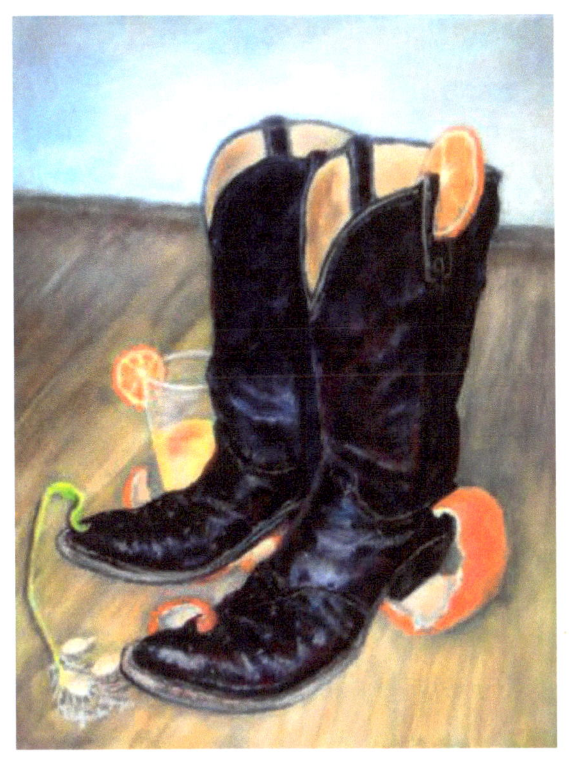

OSTRICH BULL BOOTS WITH ORANGE CRUSH SOUL

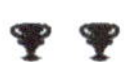

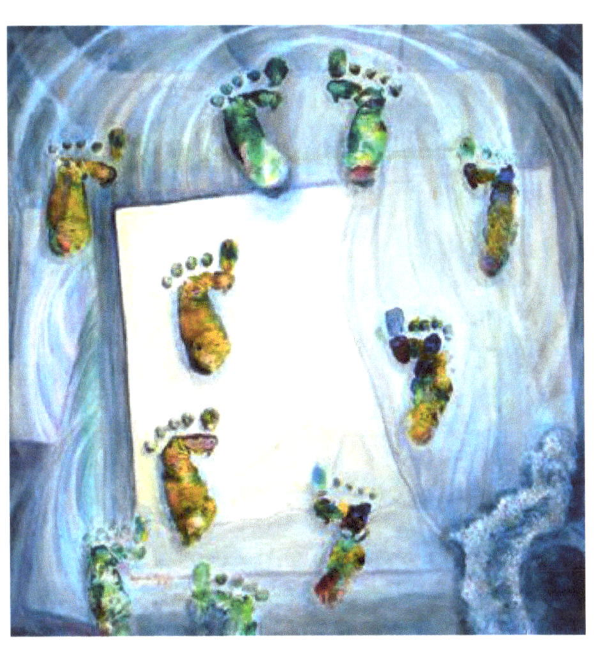

FOOTSIES AND PARADIGMS

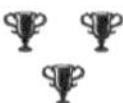

BETWEEN HUSBANDS AND WIVES GROUNDED IN LOVE
LOVE, FRIENDSHIP, TENDERNESS, MUTUAL CARE, JOY,
COLABORATION, RESPECT, HUMOR, SATISFACTION
AND A LOT OF SPACE.

BETWEEN TWO STEPS FORWARD
THE EXPECTATION OF WHAT WAS PLANNED.

BETWEEN TWO STEPS BACKWARD
THE LOSS OF WHAT COULD HAVE BEEN.

BETWEEN MY BETTER SELF AND THE PERSON THAT I WANT TO BE
A SEARCH FOR MY OWN AWAKENING.

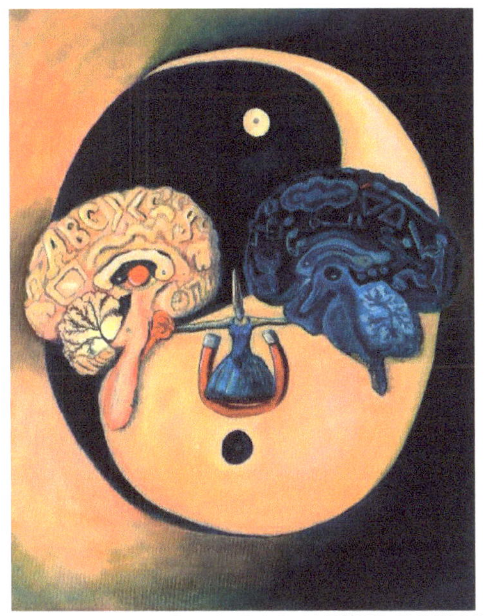

OPPOSITES ATTRACT A BALANCED DICHOTOMY

♀ ♀

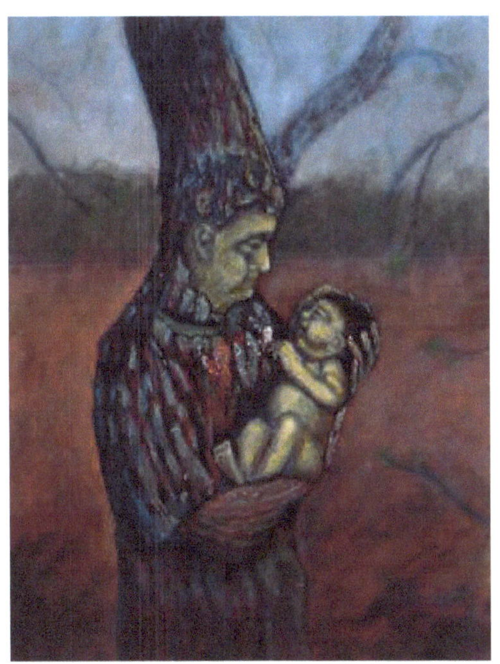

PROTECT AND DEFEND

♀♀

Ps. 3:5

"I LAID ME DOWN AND SLEPT; I AWAKED; FOR THE LORD SUSTAINED ME".

BETWEEN JOY AND SORROW
OUR SLEEPING SOUL.
JOY, HUMOR, AND SATISFACTION GLOW, WHEN JOY AWAKENS.
PAIN, AFFLICTION, AND FEAR GROW WHEN SORROW ARRIVES.
BOTH ARE INTERMITTENT PARTNERS IN OUR DAILY WALK.

BETWEEN LOVE AND HATE
DECEPTION, BETRAYAL,
SPONTANEOUS AND RECURRENT CONFLICTS,
REMORSE AND REGRETS.
A TRAIL OF BROKEN HEARTS, BROKEN HOMES AND LOST SOULS.

BETWEEN TEARS OF INFIDELITY:
LOVE, SLOWLY DROWNS.

BETWEEN BLAME AND PARDON
WITH SINCERE WILL, A SPILLAGE OF LOVE, RENEWED ENERGY
AND A PEACE INSURANCE.

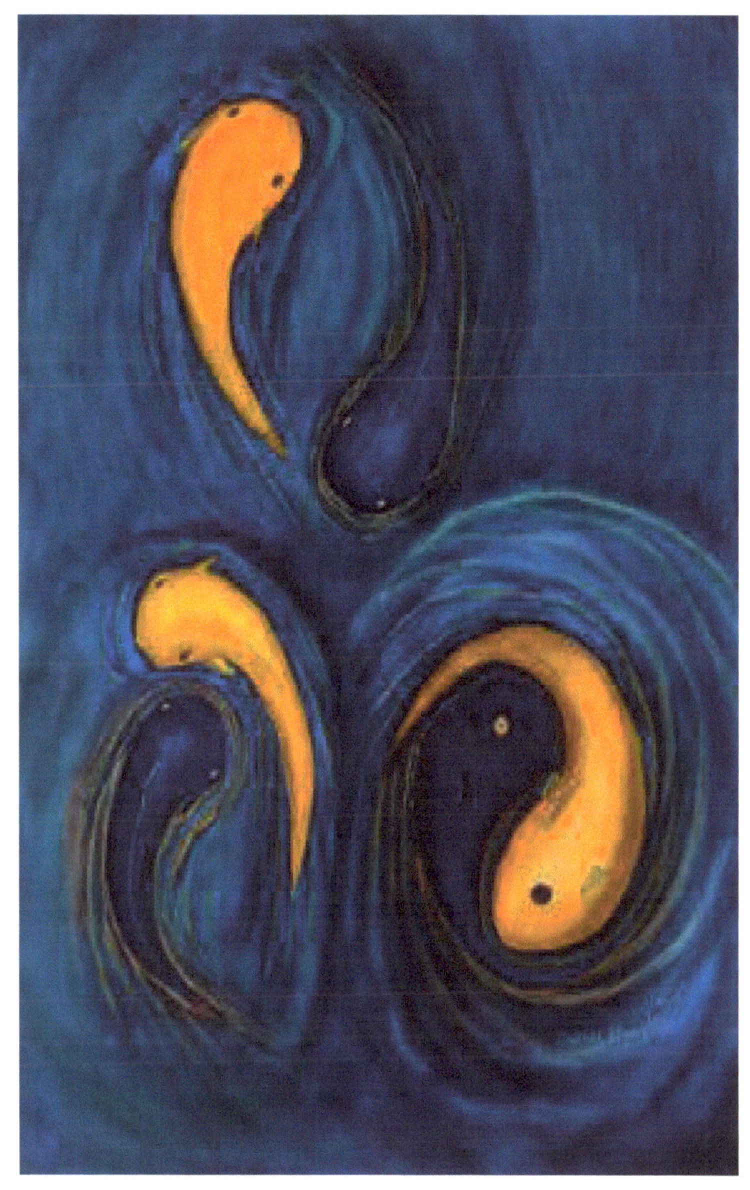

YIN & YANG MEET

♈ ♈

Col. 1:21

"AND YOU THAT WERE SOMETIME ALIENATED AND ENEMIES IN YOUR MIND, BY WICKED WORKS, YET NOW HATH HE RECONCILED".

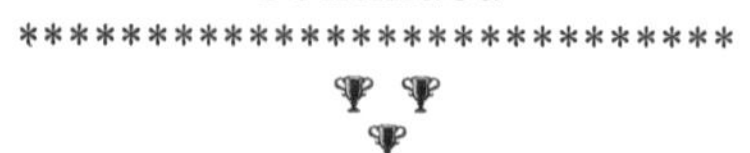

BETWEEM ENCOURAGING WORDS
HOPE IS BORN AND RAISED.

BETWEEN SPEAKING AND LISTENING
UNDERSTANDING:
IF A GOOD WILL ATTITUDE PREVAILS,
WITH FOCUSED INTENTION, A RECEPTIVE ATTENTION,
BUT ONLY, IF YOU ARE ABLE TO RECOGNIZE
THE DISTORTIONS MADE BY YOUR MENTAL FILTERS,
THAT BASED ON YOUR PREVIOUS EXPERIENCES,
AUTOMATICALLY TRY TO CHANGE YOUR PERCEPTION.

BETWEEN TRUTH AND LIES
UNLIMITED DOUBTS,
PARALIZED TRUST.

BETWEEN RIGHT AND WRONG
INTEGRITY WITHOUT UNCERTAINTY VS. DECEPTIONS & HALF
TRUTHS,
SOMNOLENCE, AND/OR AN INABILITY OR NEGLECT TO ASCERTAIN.

BETWEEN LOVE AND SCORN
THE SHARP PAIN OF INDIFFERENCE,
MOURNING FOR LOST DREAMS.

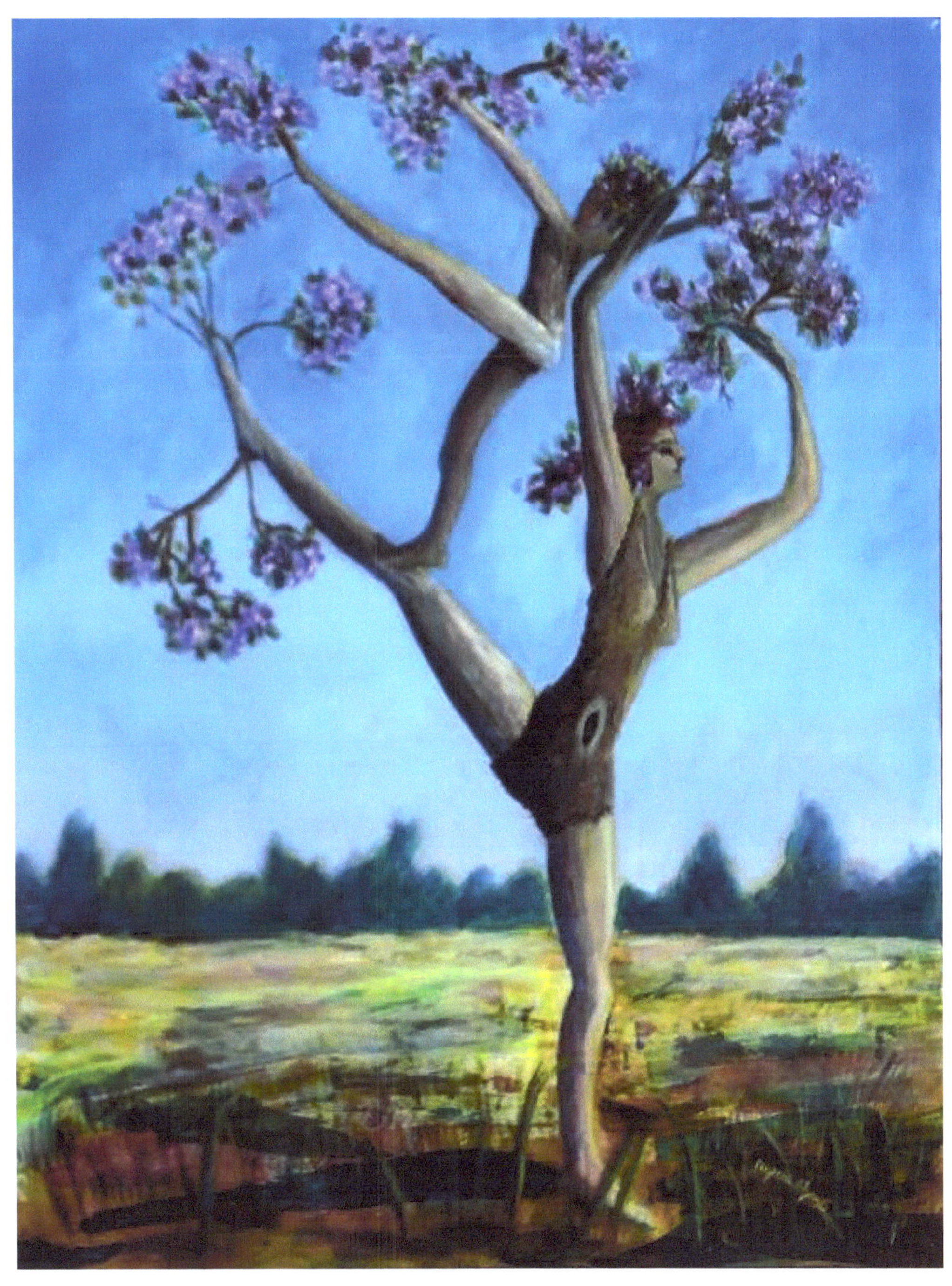

OUT ON A LIMB

♈♈

Job 37:16

"DOST THOU KNOW THE BALANCING OF THE CLOUDS, THE
WONDROUS WORKS OF HIM WHO IS PERFECT IN KNOWLEDGE?"

****

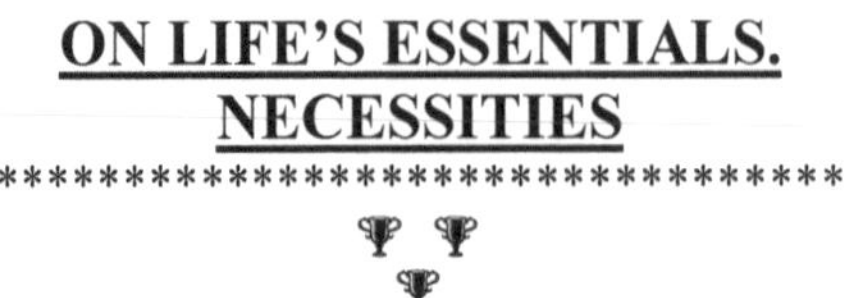

BETWEEN INHALING AND EXHALING
A BREATH, A GAS ECHANGE,
REQUISITES FOR LIFE.

BETWEEN HAIR AND FEET
FLESH, BONES, TEETH AND ENERGY.
REQUISITES FOR YOUR EXISTENCE.

BETWEEN EATING AND FIRE
INSTINCT, HUNGER, AND HABITS.
REQUISITES FOR SURVIVAL.

BETWEEN SOUP AND THE TONGUE:
APPETITE, AVAILABILITY, A SPOON, TASTE, AND ABILITY,
REQUISITES FOR THRIVING.

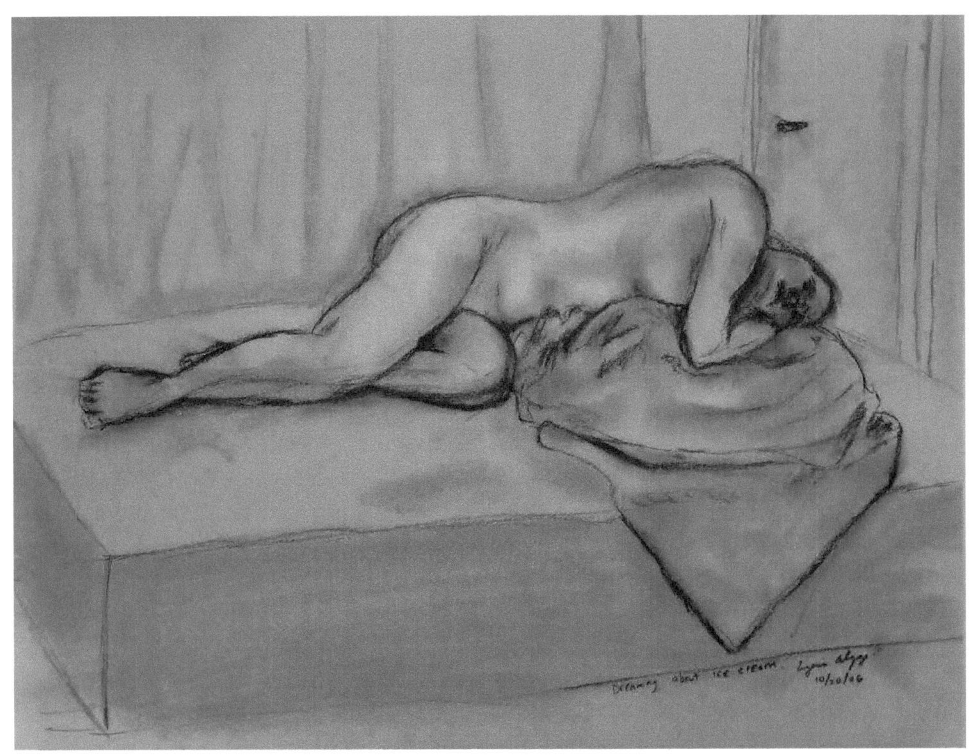

DREAMING OF ICE CREAM

🏆🏆

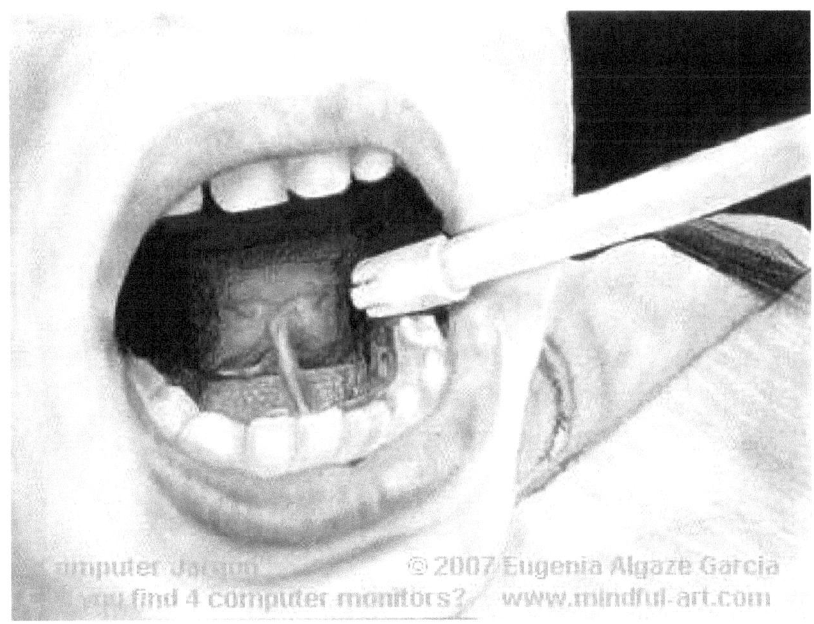

COMPUTER JARGON

🏆🏆

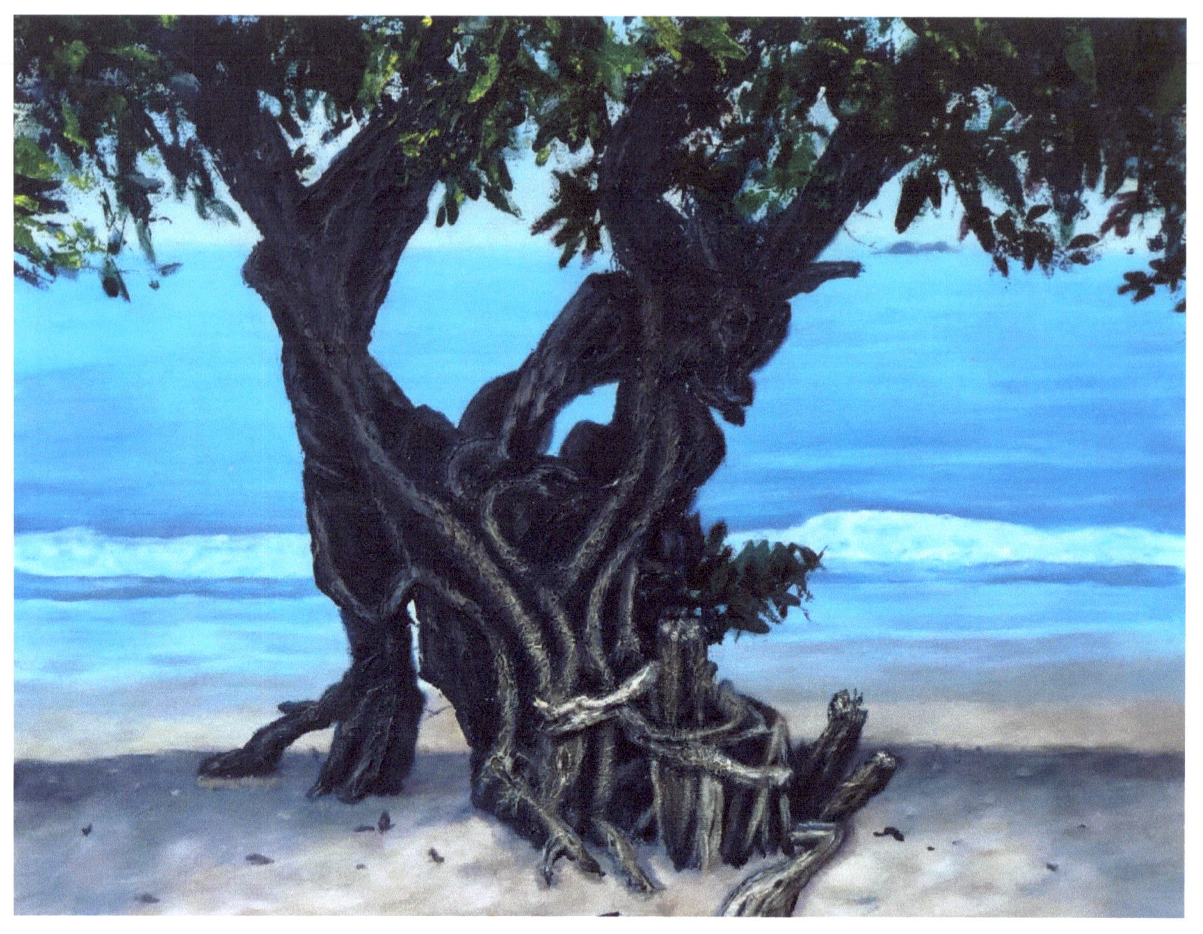

THIRSTY

Isa. 44:3

"FOR I WILL POUR WATER ON HIM WHO IS THIRSTY AND FLOODS ON
THE DRY GROUNDS:
I WILL POUR MY SPIRIT ON YOUR DESCENDANTS
AND MY BLESSINGS ON YOUR OFFSPRINGS".

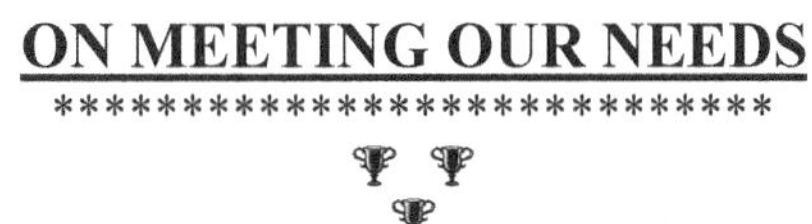

ON MEETING OUR NEEDS

****

BETWEEN THIRST, SATIATION, AND NOT DROWNNING
THE POWER OF WATER, A SEA OF COOLNESS,
WITH FLOOD POTENTIAL.
HAVING OR NOT LEARNED TO SWIM.

BETWEEN TWO SPARKS OF FIRE
FEAR OF DEVASTATION
AND
THE WARMTH OF THE HEARTH.

BETWEEN MY EXPECTATION AND THEIR OUTCOME
INTENT, FOCUS, A PLAN, DETERMINATION, A FIRST STEP,
PERSISTENCE,
PRAYERS AND MOMENTUM.

BETWEEN ENTHUSIASM AND GIVING UP
PERSISTENCE, CONSISTENCY.
LEARN TO ADAPT, LEARN WHEN TO LET GO.

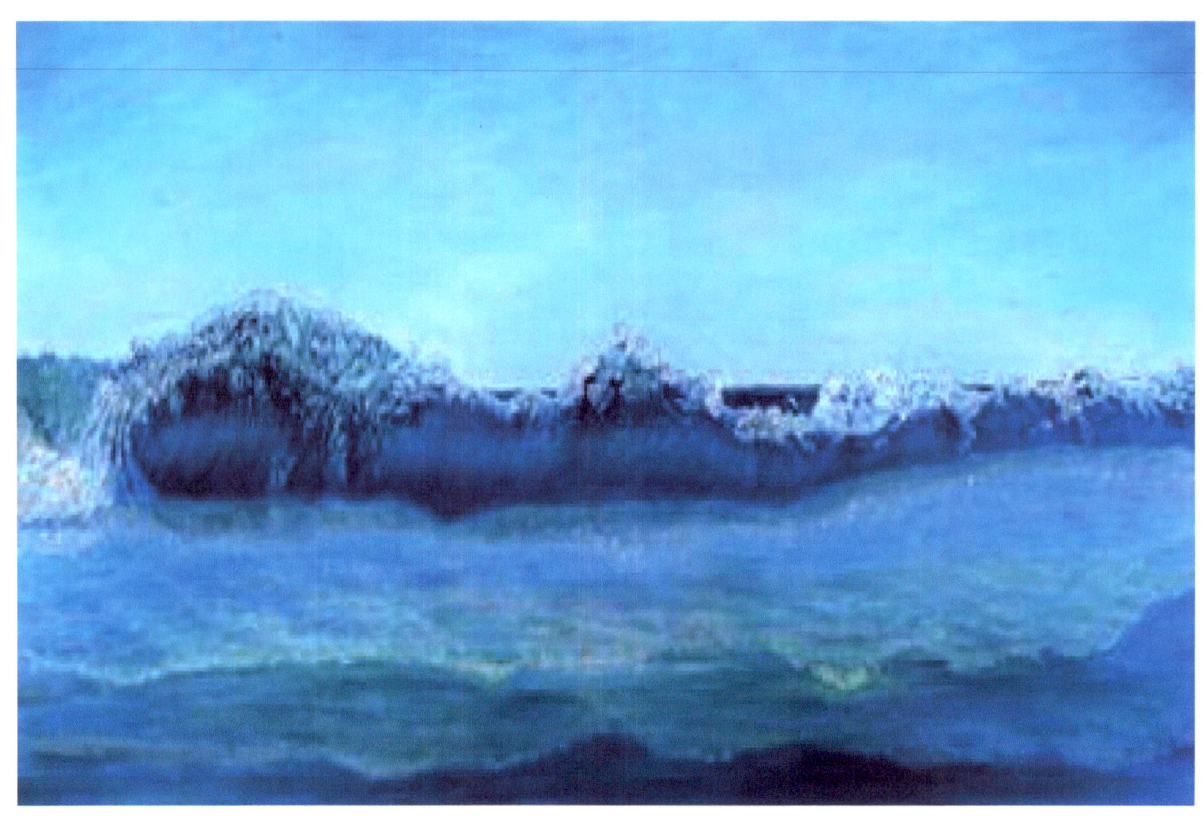

DOG PADDLING ON THE CURRENT, SHE SWIMS TO THE LEFT

ΨΨ

Prv. 3:6

"IN ALL THY WAYS ACKNOLEDGE HIM AND HE SHALL
DIRECT THY PATH"

BETWEEN WORK AND REST
EFFORT, SATISFACTION AND PRIDE IF DONE WITH LOVE,
A HEAVY DRAUGHT IF DONE WITHOUT IT.
AT THE END, RELIEF & REWARDS, MATERIAL OR INMATERIAL.
RESENTMENT AND BITTERNESS IF ABUSE HAS BEEN PERCEIVED.

BETWEEN THE PAIN OF TRAUMA AND TRANQUILITY
A WOUNDED SPIRIT WITH MEMORIES OF THE EVENT,
EXPRESSION OF THE LOSSES WITH SELF VALIDATION,
LOVE AND ACCEPTANCE. A RECOVERED INTEGRITY.

BETWEEN THE SCARS AND FORGIVENESS
A LONG JOURNEY IN A HEALING PATH,
GUIDED AND ACCELERATED BY DIVINE PROVIDENCE.

BETWEEN FEAR AND PANIC
AN OVERLOAD OF ADRENALINE,
ACCELERATED BY THE ABSENCE OF FAITH.

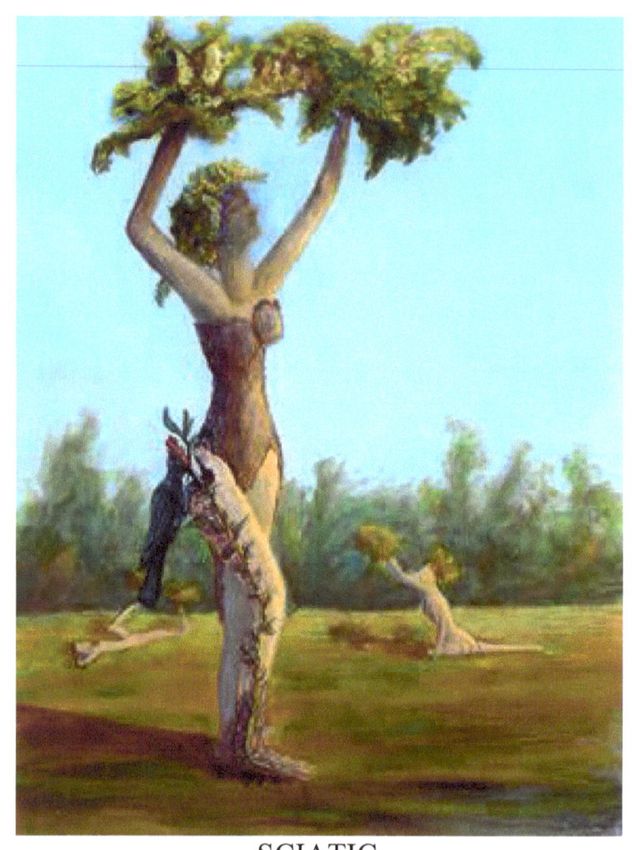

SCIATIC

♉ ♉

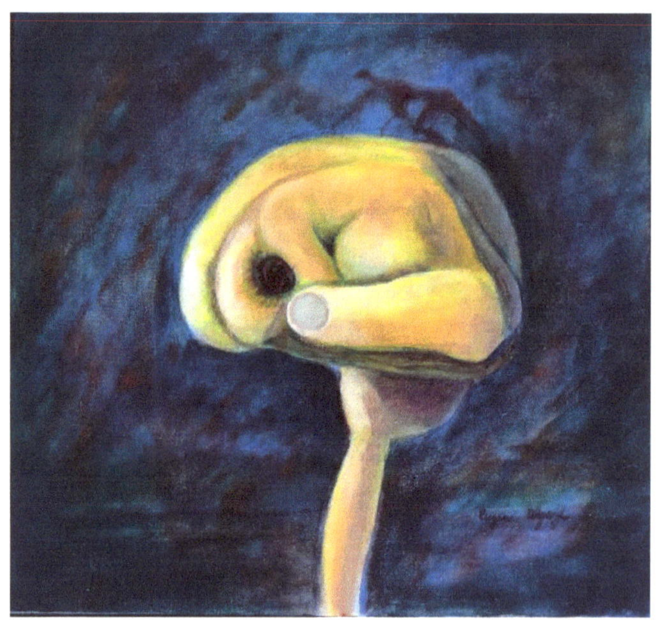

MIGRAINE HEADACHE

♉ ♉

****

BETWEEN PAIN AND HEALING
LOVE FROM WITHIN, HOPE, TOLERANCE,
APPLIED HEALTH KNOWLEDGE, FAITH,
LOVE FROM WITHOUT, POSITIVE THOUGHTS AND PATIENCE.

BETWEEN SICKNESS AND HEALTH
MORE LOVE, NURTURING, REST, REMEDIES, HEALING,
WITH TIME FOR RECOVERY.
AN UNDERSTANDING OF OUR GOD GIVEN POWER TO HEAL
AND
THE ROLE OF PRAYER.

BETWEEN A FRESH FLOWER AND A WILTED ONE
A NEED FOR WATER, LIGHT, AND NURTURING.
THE MARK OF THE PASSING OF TIME.

BETWEE MY PAIN AND OTHER'S PAIN
EMPATHY IS BORN. ANOTHER OPPORTUNITY
FOR EMOTIONAL GROWTH,
WHILE YOU ACT ON THE RELIEF OF MUTUAL PAIN.

TWO EXTREMES

☙☙

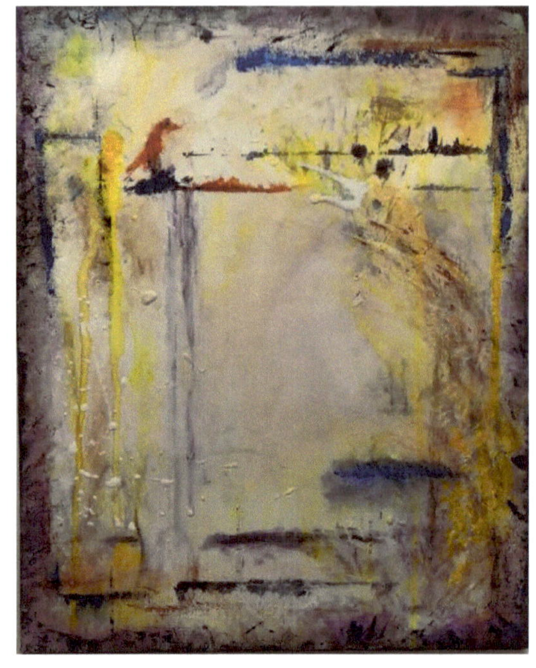

PERCHED

☙ ☙

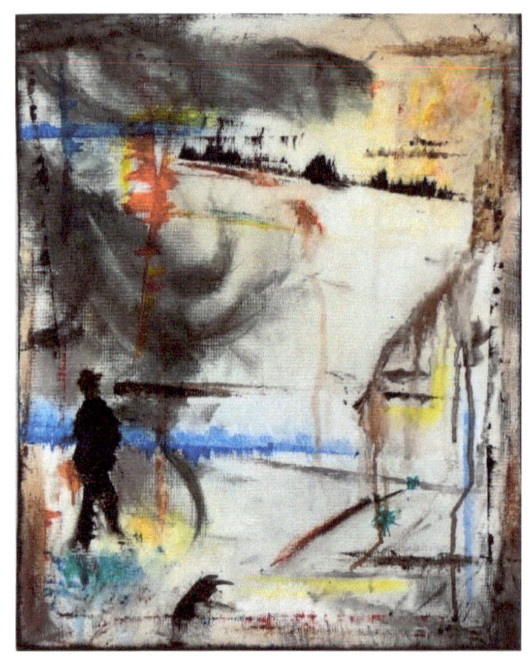

OUTER BANKS

☙☙

<u>**ON FANTASY AND REALITY.**</u>

****

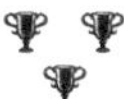

BETWEEN OUR OBJECTIVE REALITY AND THE ENTIRE UNIVERSE
A PHYSICAL MASS OF INFORMATION,
VIRTUAL REALITY OF ILLUSIONS,
HIGH SYMMETRY AND DECREASING ENTROPY.
A POSSIBLE SIMULATION?

BETWEEN FANTASY AND REALITY
A NEED TO CREATE PRETEND SITUATIONS
THAT WILL COVER OUR FEAR OF DROWNING
IN THE OCEAN OF LIFE.

BETWEEN FANTASY AND THE EDGE OF REALITY
THAT, WHICH IS NOW MOVING INSIDE OUR MINDS AND SOULS.
HYPNAGOGIC AND HYPNOPOMPIC DREAMS
MIXING WAKING AND DREAM SENSATIONS.
THE PERSISTENT CALL FOR OUR RESPONSIBILITY.

BETWEEN FANTASY AND THE CENTER OF REALITY
A MORTGAGE PAYMENT, A TOOTHACHE, A BROKEN HEART,
THE NEED TO NURTURE A LIVING BEING
IN OUR REACH OUT FOR HUMANIT.
DESCENDANCE AND TRANSCENDENCE,
REQUISITES FOR SUCCESS

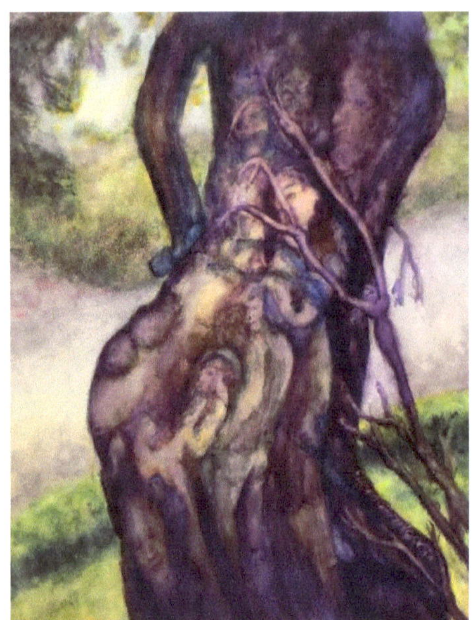

SERENDIPITY & SAGACITY

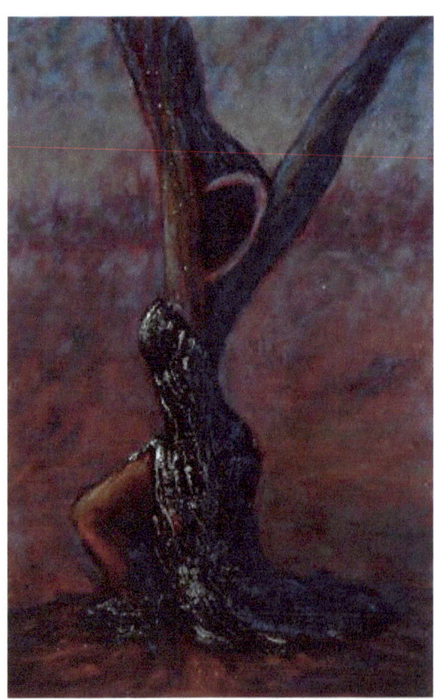

A BRIEF MOMENT OF CLARITY

ON GIVE & TAKE
****

BETWEEN LUXURY AND POVERTY
EXCESSIVE PLEASURE, UNNECESARY PAIN,
SUPPORTED BY A FALSE SENSE OF LIBERTY.

MANY IN LUXURY, MORE SO IMPOVERISHED, SOME RELIEVED,
NONE CONTENT,
INSTITUTIANALIZED GREED,
A BROKEN HUMANITY.

BETWEEN PRIDE AND ARROGANCE.
THERE IS AN EXPANDING EGO.

BETWEEN HUMBLENESS AND BOASTFULNESS
AN UNASSUMING MODEST MIND,
AN EXALTED HEART,
AND EXCESSIVE PRIDE.

BETWEEN NECESITY AND SOCIAL CONCIOUSNESS
A HUMAN NATURAL BENEVOLENCE,
LOVING EMPATHY, WITH AN ACTION PLAN FOR RELIEF,
A MASS DECISION:
(BASED ON A FORTUNOUS STROKE OF SERENDIPITY)

THE MIRACLE OF BENEVOLENCE, TURNING INTO AN ADDICTION.

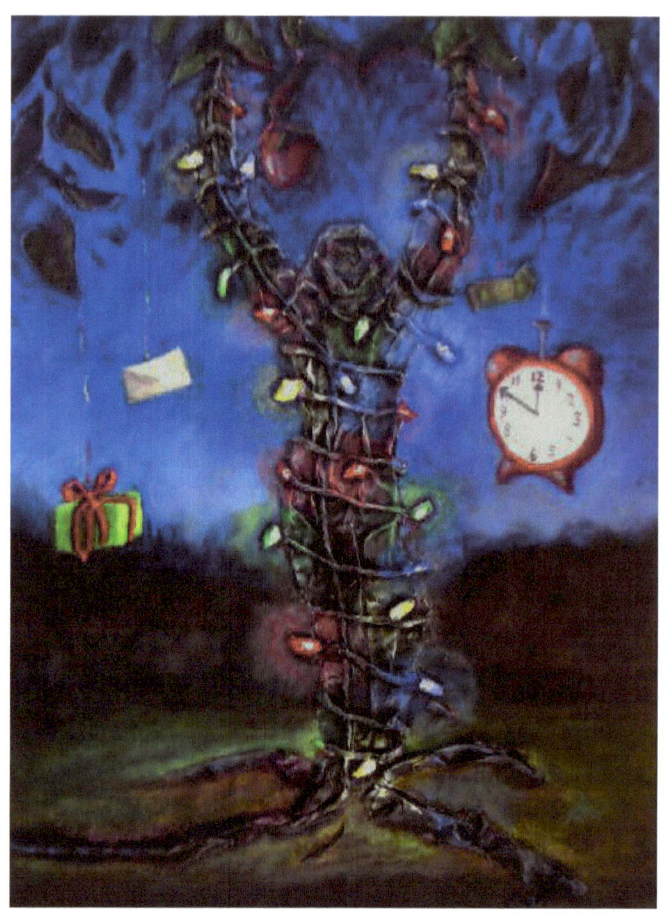

TIED UP FOR THE HOLIDAYS

♈♈

THE PROPHET BY KAHLIL GIBRAN (Pg. 42-43)

Between Slavery and Freedom: "The chains of our own binding as links of lights and shadows that cling alternatively around our minds and our souls.
And how shall you rise beyond your days and nights unless you break the chains, which you at the dawn of your understanding, have fastened around your noon hour?
In truth, that which you call freedom, is the strongest of these chains, though its links glitter in the sun and dazzle your eyes"

<u>ON MEDIOCRITY AND SUPERIORITY</u>

BETWEEN MEDIOCRITY AND EXCELLENCE
LOVE, KNOW HOW, MOTIVATION, COMMITMENT,
ACTION, PASSION, SATISFACTION
MATERIAL, SPIRITUAL AND/OR OTHER INMATERIAL REWARDS.

BETWEEN SUPERIORITY AND INFERIORITY
THE END OF THE FIGHT FOR SUPREMACY,
A HUMANITY IN ONE ACCORD
INTEGRITY, ORDER, LAWFULNESS, AND PEACE

<u>ON CRIME AND LAWLESSNESS</u>

BETWEEN AN ILLEGAL THOUGHT AND A CRIME
DENIAL OF THE DEGREE OF POTENTIAL CONSEQUENCES,
LACK OF EMPATHY WITH A SENSE OF ENTITLEMENT,
BLATANT DISOBEDIENCE TO THE LAW.

BETWEEN A CRIME AND THE TRIAL
ANGUISH, ANXIETY, LOSS OF TIME, AND MONEY. SHUNNING.

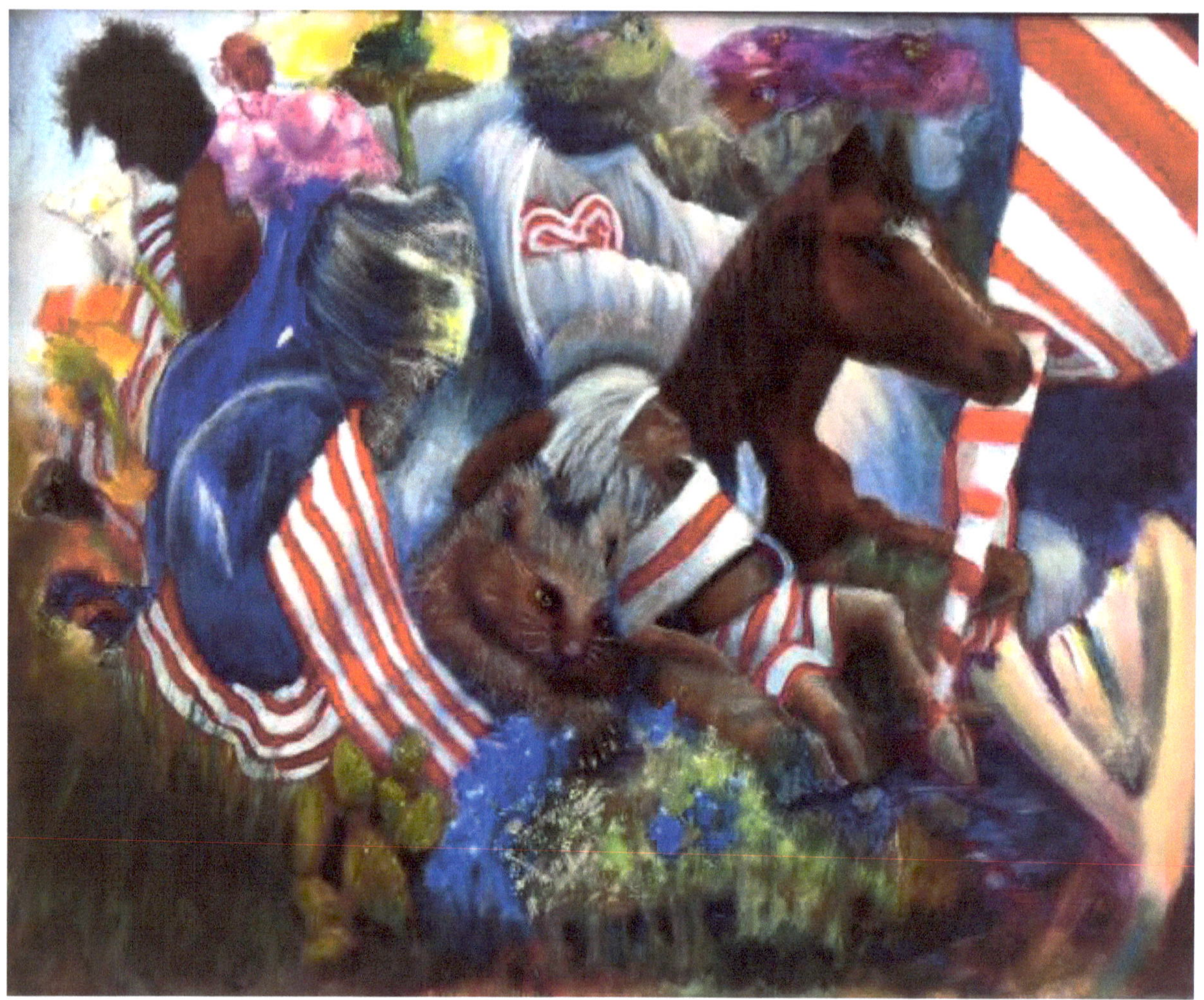

PATRIOTIC MUSINGS

Ps. 67:4

"O LET THE NATIONS BE GLAD AND SING FOR JOY! FOR THOU SHALT
JUDGE THE PEOPLE RIGHTEOUSLY AND GOVERN
THE NATIONS UPON EARTH."

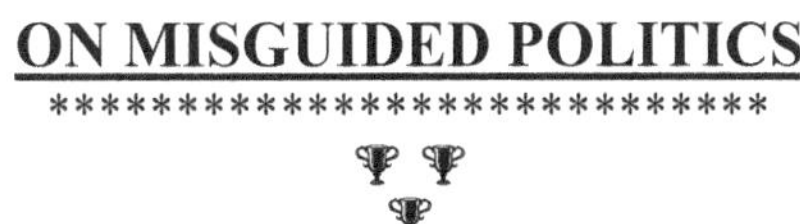

BETWEEN OPPOSING EXTREME POLITICAL PARTIES
HARKENED UNDERSTANDING,
GOVERMENTAL PARALYSIS.

BETWEEN WAR, AND WAR, AND WAR, AND ALL ONGOING WARS
EMBEDDED HABITS OF FIGHTING, TERRITORIAL ADDICTIONS,
OBSESSIONS WITH POWER,
GREED,
INSTITUTIONALIZED CRUELTY AND VIOLENCE,
DEATH,
HARMED BODIES,
WOUNDED SPIRITS, TRAUMATIZED MINDS.

BETWEEN AND OLD NUKE AND A NEW NUKE
A HISTORIC INTENTIONAL EXTERMINATION
OF INNUMERABLE LIVING BEINGS,
THE INEVITABILITY OF RE-OCCURRENCE
WITH <u>EXPONENTIAL</u> DAMAGE,
A DECREASED CHANCE
FOR THE BETTERMENT OF HUMANITY,
A CONSTANT DISDAIN OF HUMAN NEEDS,
A SHAMELESS AFFRONT TO OUR CREATOR.

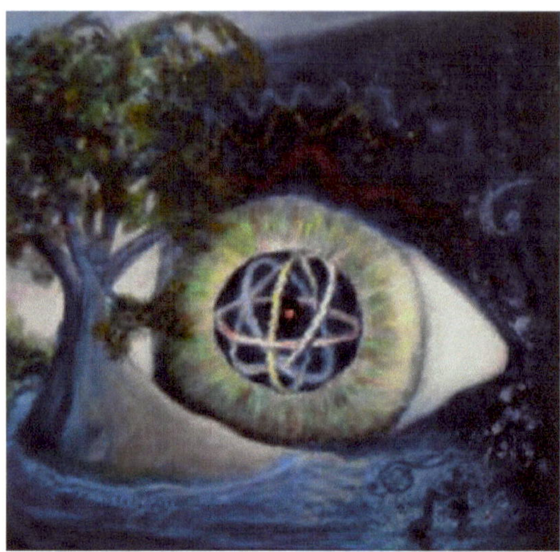

2 CORINTHIANS

2 Cor. 4:18

"WHILE WE LOOK NOT AT THE THINGS WHICH ARE SEEN, BUT AT THE THINGS WHICH ARE NOT SEEN: FOR THE THINGS WHICH ARE SEEN ARE TEMPORAL, BUT THE THINGS WHICH ARE NOT SEEN ARE ETERNAL"

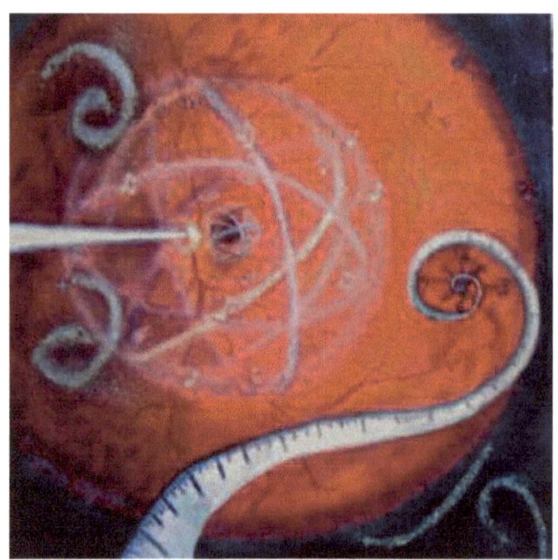

INSIDE OUT
(The side of 2 Corinthians you do not see)

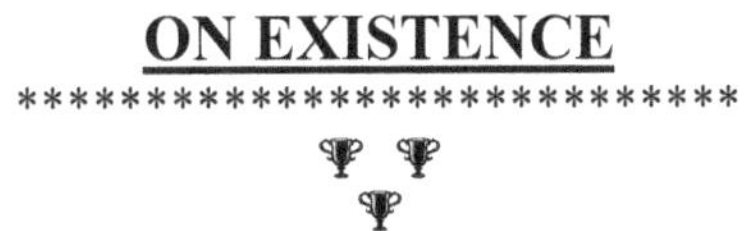

ON EXISTENCE

****

BETWEEN THE ATOM AND THE SKY
PRIMORDIAL ENERGY. OUR BREATHING SOURCE.
THE CORRELATION OF ENTANGLED PARTICLES
AND OUR HIGHEST GOALS.

BETWEEN ELECTRONS, PROTONS, WAVES AND PARTICLES
DUALITY, OBSERVATION AND SUPERPOSITION.
THE CREATION OF OUR REALITY?

BETWEEN SPACE AND TIME
A HOLOGRAPHIC UNIVERSE? THE ILLUSION OF OUR REALITY?
AN EXISTENTIAL VOID,
HOPE'S INCUBATOR?

BETWEEN POINT A AND POINT B
IN THE SPACE BETWEEN TWO PROTONS,
A WORMHOLE,
THE PARADOX OF ENTANGLEMENT,
THE POWER OF PRAYER
A NEW AND BETTER FUTURE FOR HUMANITY.

THE MONEY TREES
♈♈

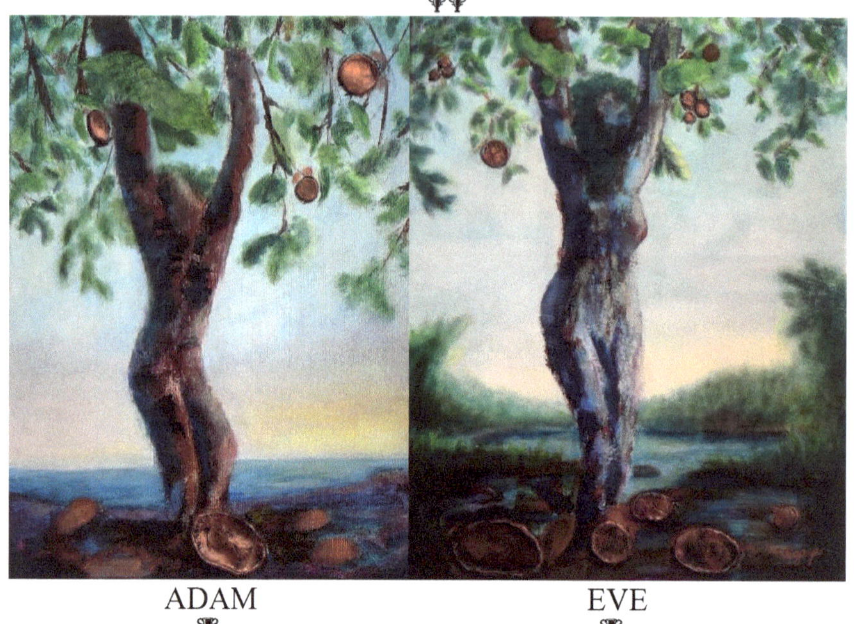

ADAM   EVE
♈   ♈

"IN GOD WE TRUST" SEEDLINGS SERIES"

♈♈

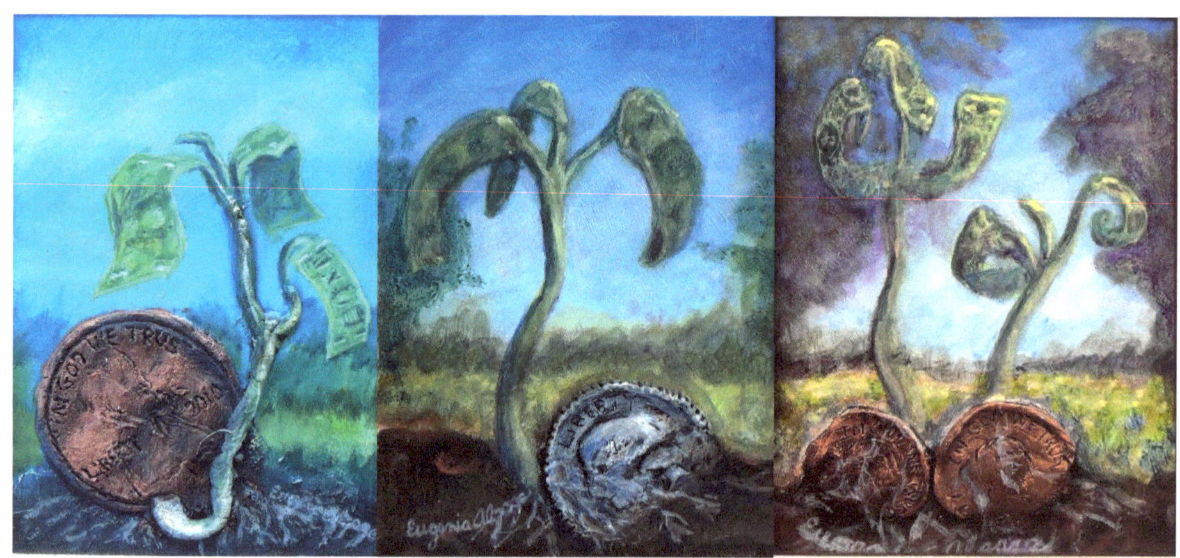

THE MONEY TREE SEEDLINGS
♈♈

THE SACRED KORAN 11:6

♈♈

"GOD -TO BE PRAISED- SAID: THERE IS NO CREATURE THAT MOVES IN
THIS EARTH WHOSE PROVISION DOES NOT COME FROM GOD."

38

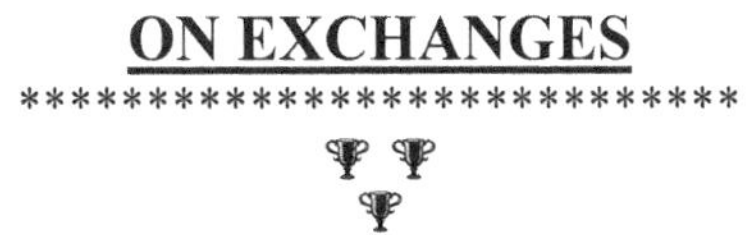

BETWEEN COMMERCIAL EXCHANGES
GREED OR ITS ABSENCE, LOVE OR ITS ABSENCE,
KINDNESS AND JUSTICE OR THEIR ABSENCE,
A POTENTIAL DOMINO EFFECT.

BETWEEN SUPPPLY AND DEMAND
NEEDS AND AVAILABILITY, PURCHASING POWER.
THE RESPONSIBILITY OF SUPPLIERS NOT TO ABUSE.
AN INDIVIDUAL RESPECT FOR HUMAN AND RELIGIOUS LAWS,
A NEW DEVELOPING SOCIAL CONSCIOUSNESS
WITH INTEGRITY AT ITS CENTER.

BETWEEN GIVING AND RECEIVING
AN UNDERSTANDING OF THE NEEDS,
A WISH AND THE ABILITY TO RELIEVE IT,
HUMBLENESS AND A BILATERAL GRATITUDE,
BECAUSE...
YOU,
HAVE BEEN DESIGNED
TO BE AN INSTRUMENT FOR CHANGE WETHER YOU ARE
THE GIVER OR THE RECEIVER.

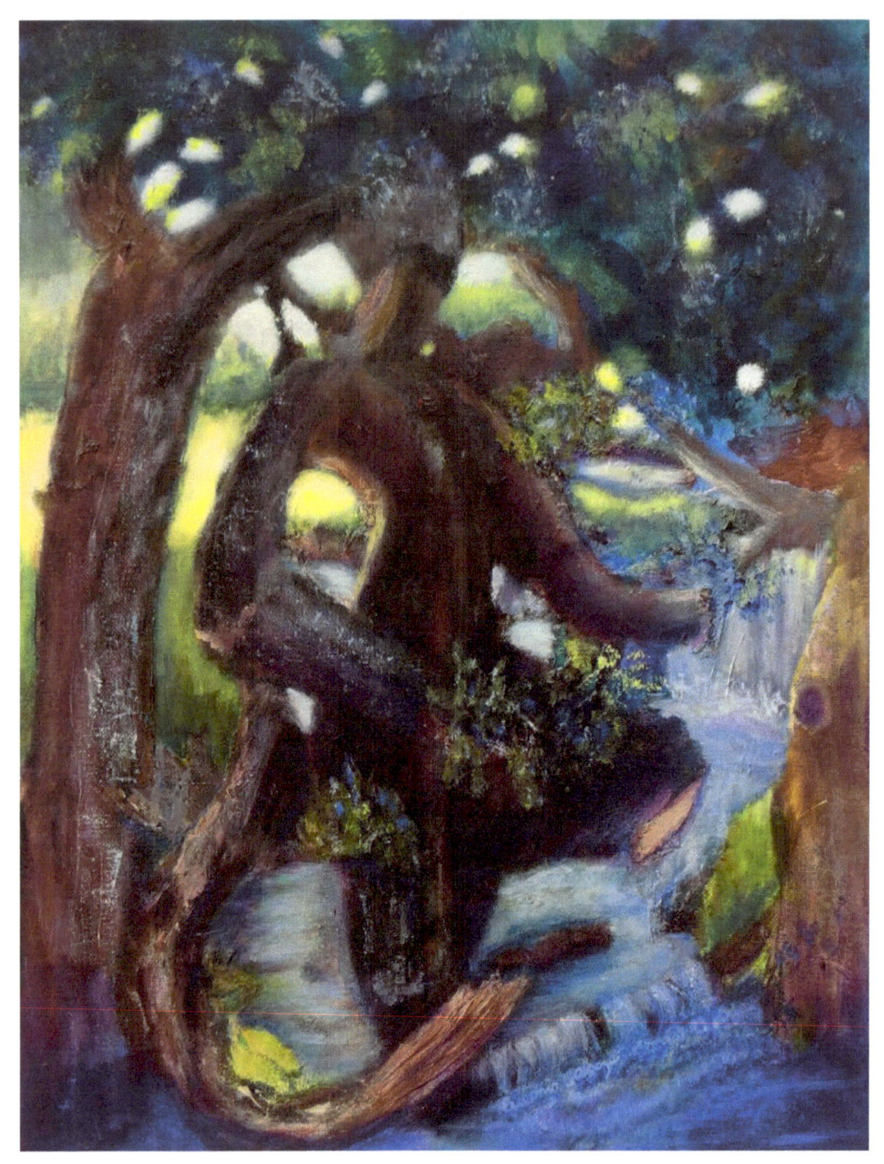

THE BALANCE GAME

🏆🏆

Job 31:6

🏆🏆

"LET ME BE WEIGHTED IN AN EVEN BALANCE
THAT GOD MAY KNOW MY INTEGRITY"

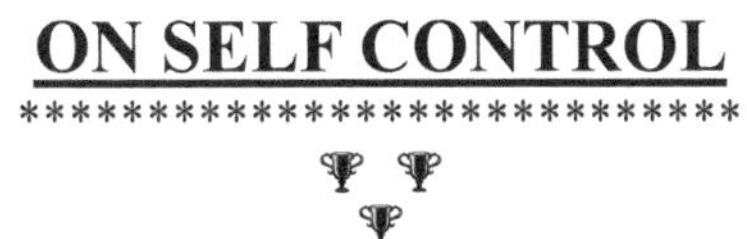

<u>ON SELF CONTROL</u>

****

BETWEEN GOOD AND EVIL
A SEA OF CONFUSION, WITH A PROPOSAL FOR CLARITY:
MAKE CHOICES, SUPPORTED BY YOUR VALUES,
WITH A DESIRE TO HAVE BOTH:
FIRST, A BETTER SELF.
SECOND, A BETTER WORLD.

BETWEEN YOUR IMPULSES AND HARMFUL BEHAVIORS
THE TACTICS THAT WE ALL USE TO AVOID TAKING RESPONSIBILITY
FOR OUR ACTIONS LIKE:

Denial, blaming, rationalization, projection, lying, self -pity, redefining, feigning, minimizing, assuming, raging, confusion, my way, I am a good guy, its mine, failure to recognize fear, etc.

(Heine, Vivian L. LMSW- ACP LSOTP & Lewis, Diana G. LPC, LSOTP
<u>Ventura Manual </u>Pgs.(30-38)

THE BAD HABIT OF NOT WANTING TO ACCEPT RESPONSIBILITY,
FOR EACH ACTION YOU DECIDE TO TAKE, OR NOT TO TAKE,
AND FAILING TO ANTICIPATE ITS CONSEQUENCES.

THE DELIBERATE BLOCKAGE OF THE KNOWLEDGE,
THAT THE DECISION,
EITHER WAY,
CAN HAVE A DIRECT EFFECT ON YOU,
BASED ON THE CONDITIONAL BIBLICAL PROMISE,
FOR AN ETERNAL LIFE.
(Mt. 25:45-46)

(Mt. 25:45-46)
♈♈

"IN AS MUCH AS YE DID IT NOT TO ONE OF THE LEAST OF THESE
(THE HUNGRY, THE THIRSTY, THE STRANGER,
THE NAKED, SICK OR IN PRISON)
YE DID IT NOT TO ME. AND THESE SHALL GO AWAY
INTO EVERLASTING PUNISHMENT.
BUT THE RIGHTEOUS, INTO LIFE ETERNAL."
♈♈

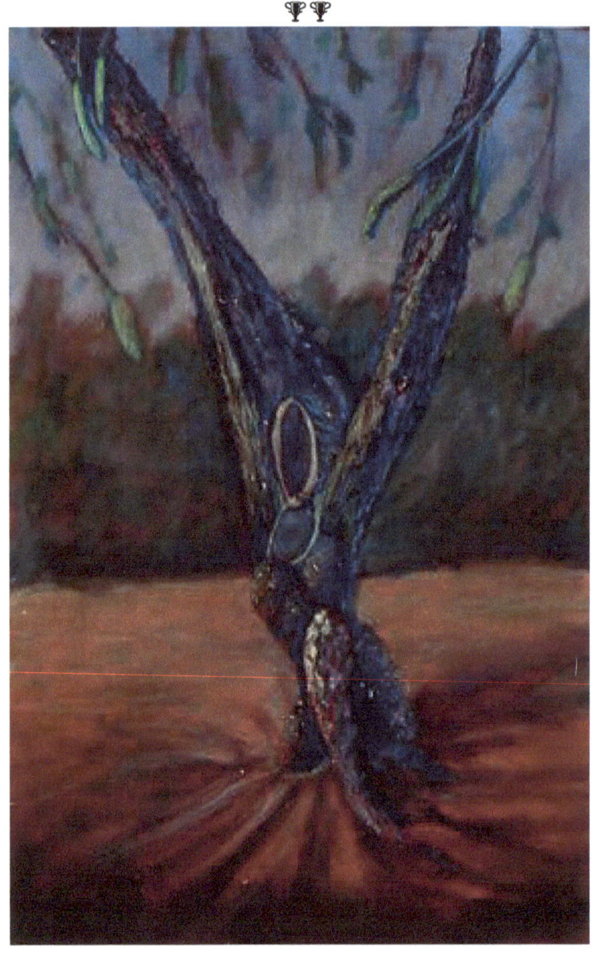

GAINING MOMENTUM

♈♈

Ps. 119: 159

♈♈

"CONSIDER HOW I LOVE YOUR PRECEPTS;
QUICKEN ME (REVIVE ME) O'LORD, ACCORDING TO YOUR LOVING
KINDNESS."

****

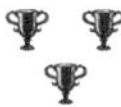

BETWEEN AN ARROW AND ITS TARGET
THE SELECTED DISTANCE IT HAS TO CROSS,
FOCUS, AIM, DIRECTION, AND ACTION.

BETWEEN INERTIA AND ACTION
THE WEIGHT OF THE OBJECT, THE FORCE AVAILABILITY,
A PURPOSE LOADED WITH POSIBILITIES.

MENTAL ENLIGHTNMENT,
WITH AN ACTION PLAN FOR YOU TO BE AN AGENT OF RELIEF.

THE NEED FOR ALL TO FOCUS ON THE DISPARITIES
THAT CAUSE PAIN AND SUFFERING.

THE RECOGNITION AND USE OF YOUR POWER TO APPLY YOUR
EFFORTS AT MICRO OR MACRO LEVELS TO IDENTIFY AND
BALANCE THESE DISPARITIES.

THE VALID ANTICIPATION OF THE POSSIBLE REALITY
OF A JUST, LOVING, CARING, EMPATHIC HUMANITY.

BETWEEN AN ALTRUISTIC IDEA AND ITS ACCOMPLISHMENT
GOALS AND OBJECTIVES,
LOVE, TRUST IN YOUR ABILITY,
HEALTH, ENERGY, PERSEVERANCE,
AND TRUST IN THE ALMIGHTY WHO IS TO GUIDE YOUR OUTCOME.

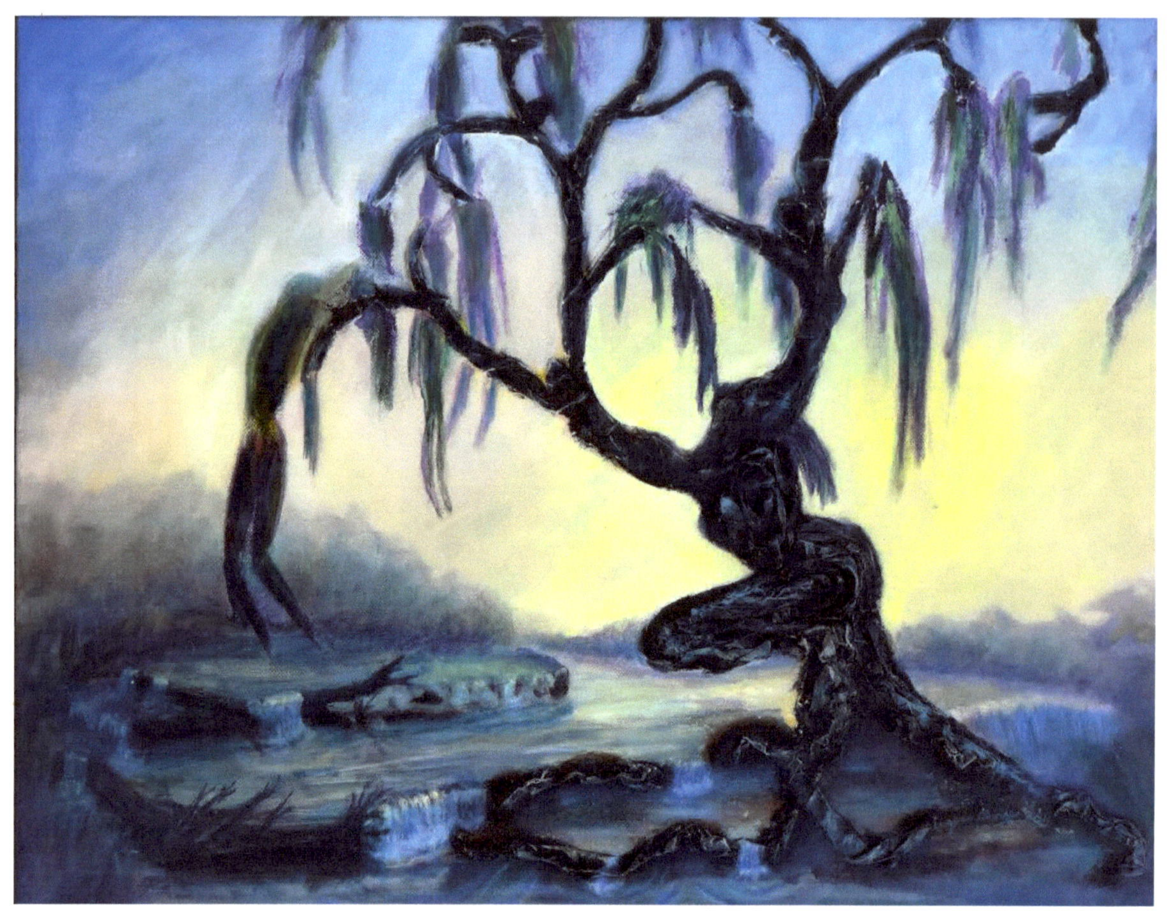

ENLIGHTENMENT

🏆🏆

Ps.18:28

🏆🏆

"FOR YOU WILL LIGHT MY CANDLE;
THE LORD MY GOD WILL ENLIGHTEN MY DARKNESS."

BETWEEN BIRTH AND DEATH
OUR LIVING SPACE.
A BREATH OF LIFE, THAT PROPELS US
AND GUIDES US IN OUR DAILY WALK,
WHERE THE POSSIBILITY OF THE JOY OF LIVING
COULD BE AVAILABLE <u>FOR ALL</u> HUMAN BEINGS.

BETWEEN PLANTING AND HARVESTING
WORK, REWARDS AND GRATITUDE:
TO THE EARTH, THE WEATHER, AND TO THE MASTERS
THAT TAUGHT YOU HOW TO CULTIVATE IT.
BUT MORESO, TO THE ONE THAT CREATED YOU,
THE EARTH, THE WEATHER AND THE MASTERS.
HE, WHO PROVIDES FOR YOU, THE OPPORTUNITY FOR YOUR
NURTURING, SHELTERING AND EXISTENCE.

BETWEEN DEATH AND ETERNITY
JOY OR REGRETS,
AN UNCERTAIN SPACE FOR INQUIRY.
AND.... THEN
WHEN IT'S ALL OVER,
BETWEEN THE FINAL SIGHT AND DEATH,
A DETACHMENT OF THE MIND AND....THE HOPE OF IMMORTALITY.

"To be, or not to be? That is the question".
(First line of <u>Hamlet's</u> Soliloquy)

♈♈

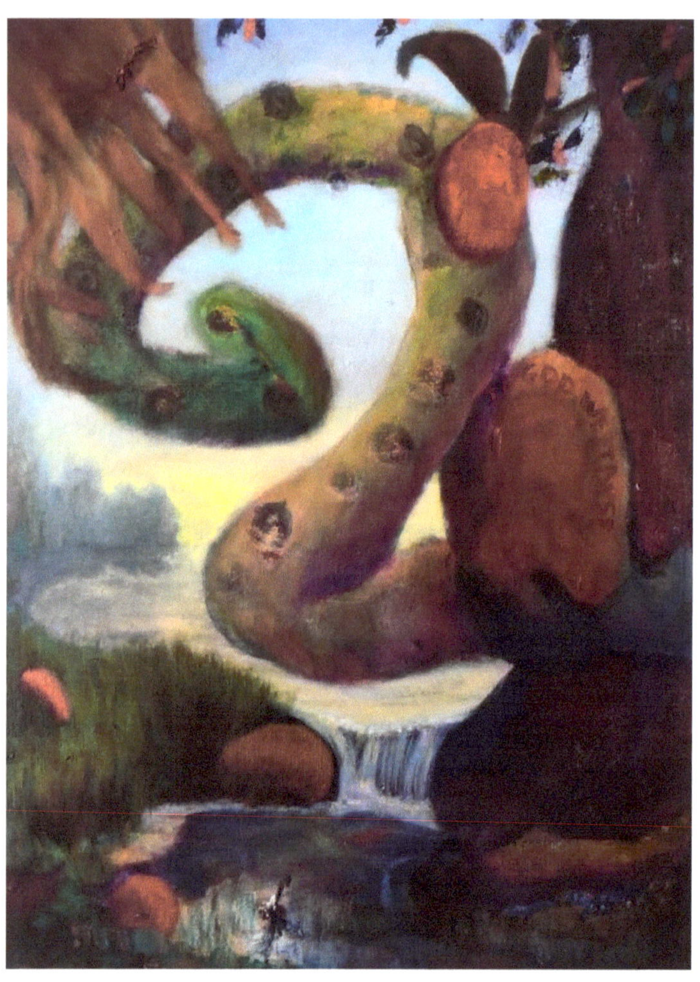

ENIGMA

♈♈

"To do, or not to do? That is the question."
(Closing line of <u>Inner Space Awakening</u>...)

Ezq.17:10

♈♈

"YEA, BEHOLD, BEING PLANTED, SHALL IT PROSPER?
SHALL IT NOT UTTERLY WITHER,
WHEN THE EAST WIND TOUCHETH IT?

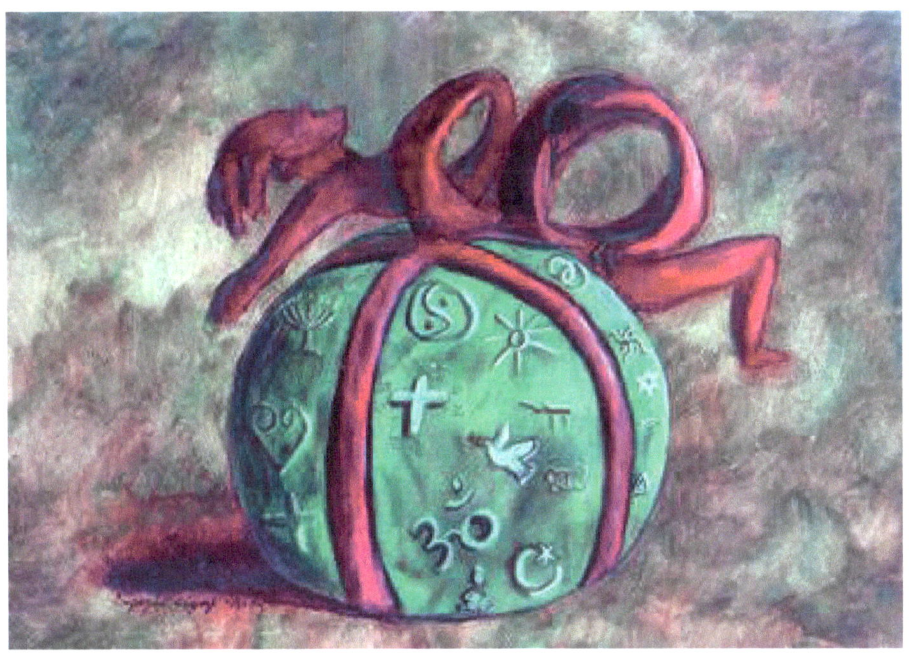

SPIRITUAL LABOR BEARING PEACE
(LABOR, OF LOVE)

ΨΨ

A Note by the Artist

ΨΨ

"Spiritual Labor Bearing Peace" The idea of a Spiritual birth for the birth of peace was inspired by the Holidays and the similarities between a difficult natal labor, and the difficulties world leaders are having to obtain and maintain peace. This is a past and still present reality. The large variety of races, languages, cultures, historical backgrounds, political systems and religions has prevented this to happen. Love and peace, although hidden, are present, only to be found, delivered, shared, and activated, in a joined "Labor of Love" that starts at the individual level."

**MAY PEACE BE
A CONCEIVED, NURTURED APPLIED AND SUSTAINED REALITY.**

HOW COULD <u>YOU</u> MAKE IT HAPPEN?

ABOUT THE AUTHOR

❦❦

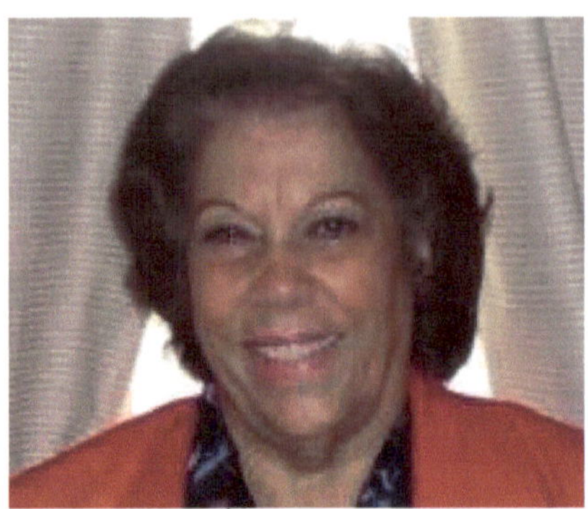

TERESA PIQUÉ ALGAZE – ESPINOZA
M.S.W. L.C.S.W.

❦❦

Teresa Piqué Algaze -Espinoza is a behavior / trauma psychotherapy specialist who uses Art Therapy techniques and Spiritual Counseling with other therapies, for deeper healing in her practice. Now partially retired, she has time and energy to cultivate and apply her bilingual writing abilities, her personal, and professional experiences with her academic knowledge. Doña Tere, a term of endearment used by her clients is a Cuban-American who came to the USA, as a refugee in her teenage years. She studied at the University of Connecticut receiving her undergraduate degree with a Major in Psychology and a minor in Latin American Studies, in the early 70's, getting her Masters in Social Work from the University of Houston, in Houston, TX., in the early 80'. For ten years she worked as a psychotherapist in mental health settings: both in-patient and out-patient and for three years as a Clinical Director and Deputy Director of The Chicano Family Center, of a multiservice nonprofit agency in SE Houston. In 1993, she founded Arena Counseling Center Inc., where she was President, CEO and Psychotherapist. With an Emotional Trauma specialty and two required licenses, Arena Counseling Center Inc served both, victims and perpetrators of abuse through State of Texas and Harris and Ft. Bend County serving more than 9,000 clients through her contracts and subcontractors, from 1993 to 2021. She is a member of the National Association of Social Workers.

Her thoughts and poems have a deep spiritual component that transcends Judeo-Christian boundaries.

Piqué-aze Productions
©2024

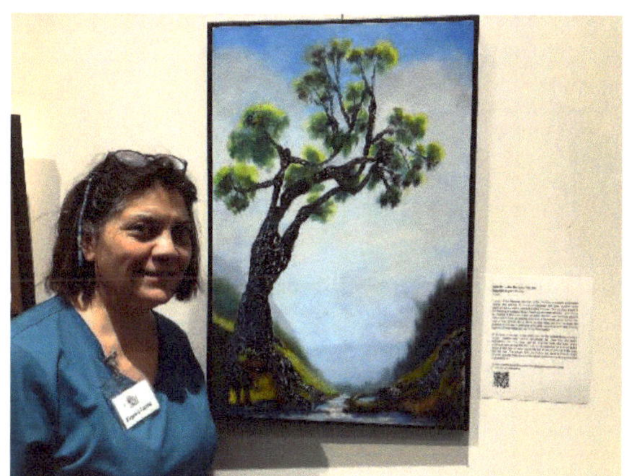

EUGENIA ALGAZE GARCIA
B.B.A. M.B.A. N.S.A.

Eugenia Algaze Garcia is an award-winning artist and a life time member of the NSA (National Society of Artists) who uses her imagination as a medium and creates art in ink, acrylic, watercolor, graphite, soft pastels, and mixed media, reflecting energy she perceives from her subjects, she creates meaningful artworks with hidden imagery to represent multiple facets of her subject's interests. Her style was developed from over 40 years of observations of the hidden beauty in the world around us; learning skills from many other artists, while applying them with constant practice, love and passion, toward her creations of Mindful Art works.

In her early years, she was influenced by art teachers in Hartford CT. where she was born and raised, during exercises of shape recognition of letters and hidden symbols in shapes and colors. She was also impressed by Dr. Seuss creative spins on reality. Her family's love for art, in addition to an art gene manifesting itself in each generation, facilitated her early art exposure at the Wadsworth Atheneum Museum, where she discovered the great masters, their characteristics and painting styles: da Vinci's knowledge and curiosity of how things work; Salvador Dali's surrealism and use of symbols that foster thinking. It was this latter one that most influenced her painting style, while they all stimulated her boundless creativity.

Thinking that her passion for the arts would require a financial backing, she pursued a career path in accounting earning a B.B.A. from Texas A&M University in College Station. She worked in public accounting and then in the private sector for a time, during which she received her CPA license from the State of Texas. She earned an M.B.A, from University of Houston at Clear Lake, exercising her career until she stayed home to raise her two children. In 2003, her dream, of art, as a career, became a reality.

Through over four decades of experimentation, studying and persistent exercises to continuously improve her art expression, Eugenia has been able to enhance her early art exposure with fine art skills she has gained through: art courses, workshops, books, and many hours of practice to develop her style for her growing business: Mindful Art. Multiple Streamline Art Videos, and livestreamed video workshops (like Eric Rhoads daily "Art School Live" broadcasts) have been an ongoing training source during the COVID and post COVID years, further enhancing her skills.

Eugenia Algaze Garcia's <u>Mindful Art</u> style involves a mix of impressionistic realism, symbolism, abstraction and surrealism as she interprets images and ideas from her mind using "left and right brain" art techniques to communicate visually. Garcia's art has also been influenced by a near death experience in childhood, being a wife, mother, grandmother and by the Psychology, learned from her mother, a Psychotherapist in TX.

As an art teacher, her classes are inspiring and instructive, stimulating the student's creativity. Numerous exhibitions plus her generous community involvement, have exposed her as a recognized and notable artist. Support from other artists, new patrons, friends, and family have provided emotional fuel for her artistic development.

She began teaching homeschoolers in 2008 basic art skills and how to think like an artist. This was followed by requests to teach more art classes. Some of her youth and adult art students have won awards for their art in competitions.

Garcia's art has received recognition locally, nationally, and internationally She currently teaches and exhibits her art at Fort Bend Art Center in Rosenberg, TX, and other art venues. Eugenia is a life time member of the National Society of Artists, with Signature Status since 2010. She belongs to the Art League of Fort Bend, Lone Star Art Guild, Fort Bend Art Center, and Dreamline Artists.

LIST OF <u>MINDFUL ART</u> WORKS IN   <u>INNER SPACE AWAKENING</u>
WITH: SIZE, ART MEDIUM, DATE AND FILING SOURCE

❦❦

Pg. #

❦❦

51

Eugenia Algaze Garcia
www.mindful-art.com
www.facebook.com/Mindful.Art.Eugenia.Algaze.Garcia

Piqué-aze Productions
© 2024

<u>CONCLUSION</u>

The art work selected to be the back cover of this book shows images of living beings who appear to be at peace with themselves and their surroundings reflecting a sense of wellbeing that results from expanding the mind, while generating new perspectives. Could it be a future reflection of our readers?

It is by cultivating awareness, studying, meditation and prayer that a spiritual awakening can take place, where individuals can have a profound shift in their understanding of themselves, each other, and their environments.

There must be a motivation for change, and a decrease of experiential avoidance. What could be preventing you from developing altruistic goals that could make you a better person, your family a better family, your neighborhood a safer place and this earth a better world? It is also important to discover and clear unclear values and believes, to base thoughts and actions on a solid ground, where commitments could be anchored. Acceptance and compliance with your beliefs, and/or religious laws, may provide a steady path to follow, without losing site of that Universal Divine Essence which could serve as a common denominator as well as a unifying power source.

Art and poetry have been used as a tool to awaken awareness. If we have entertained you while motivating you to make a direct impact on the betterment of humanity, then we have fulfilled our purpose.

<u>**RECOGNITIONS**</u>

☙❧

I would like to express my gratitude:

- To my daughter Eugenia for her collaboration and assistance providing the art for the supportive structure of this book, and the technical assistance for the culmination of this project, despite her busy time painting, teaching, and fulfilling her community and family responsibilities.

- To my grandsons: Nicolas and Alexander Garcia who provided proofreading time for the English portions of this book, as well as intellectual feedback from the perspective of the Millennials.

- To my husband Marco Antonio Espinoza, for his support and understanding during the many family hours used to complete this work.

- To the many colleagues, subcontractors, and private and governmental agency workers that I worked with and clients that I served, through 23 years in my Psychotherapy practice, The Arena Counseling Center Inc. in Houston, TX. It was there where I was able to expand my academic knowledge about the human condition in its many facets and where the awakening of my own inner space began to manifest itself through the multiplicity of shared real-life situations that required discernment, at the deepest levels, on a daily basis.

- To the Highest Power that inspired me after a few months of silence, prayer and meditation, providing the middle ground of concepts and possibilities, which created the substance for the poem The In-Between, backbone for this book.

- To Dr. Kenneth Ring, University of Connecticut Professor Emeritus of Psychology, who introduced me through a course in Social Psychology/Interpersonal Psychology in 1974, where Altered States of Consciousness achieved through meditation, served to access the Universal Quantum Consciousness then not yet labeled. Without his contribution, this book would not have been possible.

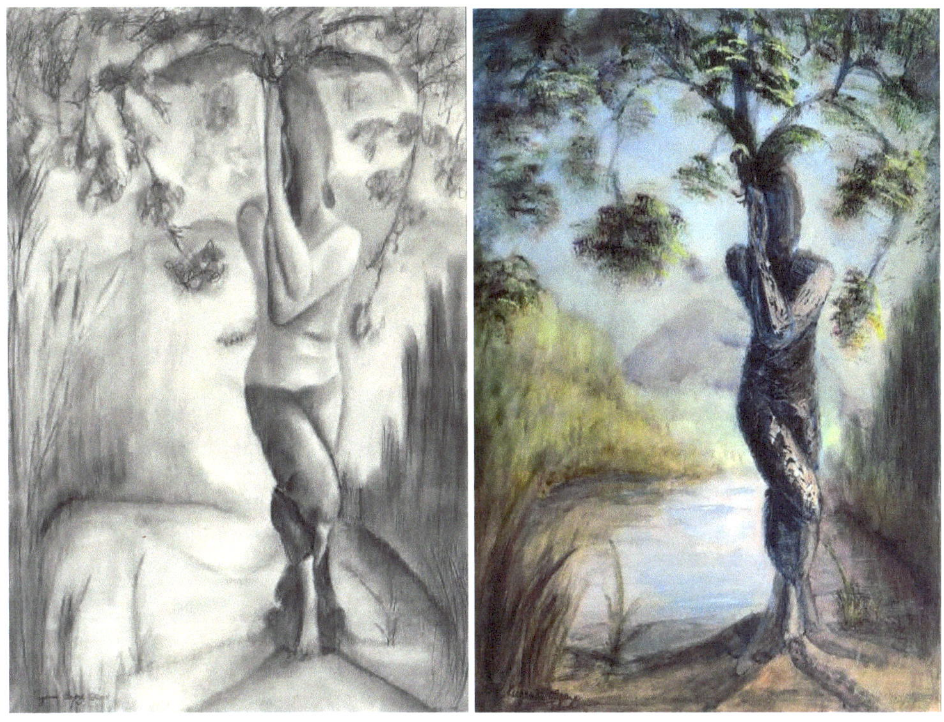

YOGA TREE EAGLE POSE-ACRYLIC

Ψ Ψ

Both of these are inspired by the yoga pose, Eagle. The pencil one, was a study for the one in acrylic.   In addition to the not-so-"hidden" person that functions as a tree trunk doing the yoga pose, there is at least one eagle hidden in each as well as a person praying, where the praying hands join to form the base of each tree.

BOOK DESCRIPTION

Have you ever wondered about the ways of thinking, that still in the 21st Century, keep individuals and their partners, employers and employees, religious systems, and some nations, fighting, with each other, without an apparent solution?

In this book, a mental health trauma specialist presents capsules of wisdom to stimulate thinking, clarify perceptions, and possibly influence the reader to think, search for and apply, new creative solutions for his/her life situations and environment.

Brief thought expressions are nestled, categorically, in a framework of alternating colorful, thought-provoking original paintings, by her world recognized artist daughter, as well as a few selected spiritual quotations, from Judeo-Christian & Islamic traditions. This author also reflects her exposure to Hindu and Buddhist thinking as well as mindfulness-based meditation.

**Reading this book, you are to enjoy a unique,
entertaining, absorbing, stimulating practical experience!**

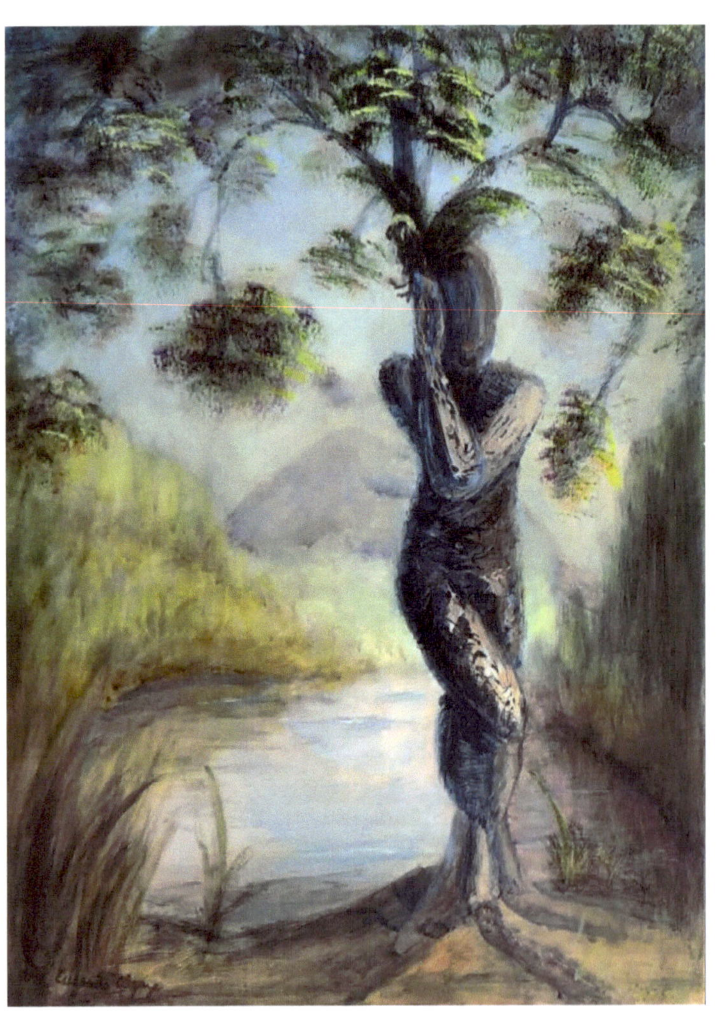